COP TALES

Legends, Pranks and Stories from a Bygone Era

I0483874

James H. Lilley

© **2015 by James H. Lilley**

All rights reserved. No part of this book may be reproduced, stored in a retrieval system or transmitted in any form or by any means without the prior written permission of the publishers, except by a reviewer who may quote brief passages in a review to be printed in a newspaper, magazine or journal.

First printing.

Cover Design by Melissa "Missy" Wrobleski

Introduction

The men and women who live and work within the law enforcement community reside in a world that is often filled with tales of horror and heartbreak. Yet, as strange as it might seem, that world is, or at least was, just as often loaded with episodes of practical jokes, outrageous perverted humor and strange, but true stories. Of course, those of us who have worn, or still wear, the badge, fully understand the bizarre goings on, because we know it is simply one of the ways to hold on to what's left of our sanity.

From verbal barbs to elaborate jokes, humor was a part of our job. Long before "politically correct, warm and fuzzy, and Oh Dear God forbid that we offend even a single person" came into practice, nothing was sacred to those behind the badge. It was open season, with no bag limit, on every topic from mothers, wives, sweethearts, fathers, sisters, brothers, sons, daughters, your dog, cat, goldfish, parakeet, race and religion. It wasn't until a minority of limp dicks appeared in the ranks that our brand of police humor was considered, insensitive and off limits. In spite of limp dicks, with nothing but politically correct views and aspirations of personal gain, humor is alive and well within the law enforcement community. Although today's brand of police humor is probably tame compared to that of the "Dinosaur Generation."

The stories you are about to read are true, but please keep in mind that what you are about read also happened in another era. Things were very different back then and I believe we were much closer knit in those days. We watched out for each other, regardless of the color of our uniforms or organizations we represented.

Dedication

This work is dedicated to the men and women of the local, state and federal law enforcement agencies, who have devoted their lives to protecting and serving their community. It is for the families who wait at home while their loved ones answer the call of their chosen profession, and to the memory of all of those who made the ultimate sacrifice while proudly wearing our badge of honor.

Acknowledgments

My sincere thanks to all of you who took time to contribute to this work. I look forward to the opportunity to gather around a table with you again and set the stage for another voyage into the world of police pranks and perverted humor.

Thank you to Dean Clark, my computer wizard, who has always been there to bail me out when my computer "skills" seem to malfunction.

Thank you to Melissa "Missy" Wrobleski for your time, effort and artistic skills designing the cover.

To Jody, my loving and very patient wife, thank you for your love and support and those never ending words of encouragement.

The Gooney Monster

Griff Jones, Denny Laumann, Karl Beazley, Joe Collins,
Jim Robey and Jim Lilley

The region between Murray Hill and Kindler Roads located in what is now Columbia, Maryland, in years long gone, was nothing more than an expanse of grass covered fields and hills, farmlands and hundreds of acres of trees and flowing streams.

It was back in those days (days before cell phones) that a mysterious telephone call to the police sparked panic and curiosity. The anonymous caller reported seeing a Sasquatch-like creature cross Murray Hill Road at the bridge and walk down into the streambed. Responding officers found nothing that even vaguely resembled a displaced Yeti, or Big-foot and declared the call a hoax.

A second and third call was received, but on these occasions the callers gave their names and addresses and asked to speak with an officer. Within a few days, dozens of calls came into the police, reporting sightings of a strange creature on Kindler Road as well as Murray Hill Road, and always near the bridges or streambed on those roads. Descriptions of the beast were varied, and ranged from the Sasquatch-like creature to a thing that appeared to be part bird, part humanoid and very large.

What was thought to be a hoax was turning Murray Hill and Kindler Roads into highways for the curious. Friday and Saturday nights, which until the calls began, had been uneventful along the old, narrow, country roads, turned into bedlam. Cars lined both sides of those roadways as far as the eye could see in all directions and hundreds of people, from teens to grandparents, with everything from flashlights to lanterns were standing on the bridges, hoping to catch a glimpse of what was now dubbed "The Gooney Monster."

Police were called to clear the traffic jams, but soon the tales of the wild beast brought added headaches for law enforcement officers. The Friday and Saturday night mobs were now bringing firearms to protect themselves. Shotguns and rifles were being openly carried and, although no handguns had been observed, it was a certainty that someone had to be packing a concealed revolver or semi-automatic.

On a cool Friday evening in late fall, Jim Robey and I were cruising along Murray Hill Road in our unmarked car. As we neared the bridge, we saw a man casually walking down the center of the road, carrying a shotgun. We stopped the man, identified ourselves and confiscated his shotgun—not that it was against the law, but because of the hazard presented to the others overrunning the entire area. We made a quick check of the cars parked near the bridge, and located two additional shotguns and a rifle lying in the grass.

Of course, no one claimed ownership of the weapons and we hauled them to the police station where their rightful owners later claimed them.

Nothing swayed local residents and the idle curious from their belief that some large, hairy or feathered beast was running amok in Howard County. The saga of "The Gooney Monster" was growing by the day. Rumors were circulating through local high schools that the creature had abducted several teenaged girls. Yet, the police had not taken a single report of a missing or kidnapped teenaged girl. There were wild yarns of human skeletal remains being discovered along the streambeds, but state and local police were not investigating any such mysteries. Calls also began to come in from residents "up stream of the monster's normal habitat" stating that it was lurking in their back yards near the tree line.

"The Gooney Monster" would not go away.

Just after noon on a Friday, I parked my car on Murray Hill Road and walked down into the streambed, determined to put the monster tale to rest. In no time at all, I found a colorful dress that someone had shredded and very carefully placed partially in the stream. The portion on the embankment had a large rock, which was almost perfectly centered, holding it in place. I pulled it out of the stream, rolled it into a ball and carried it back to my car.

I spent almost two hours wandering along the banks of the stream, noticing from time to time what appeared to be someone's attempt to leave "monster footprints" in the soft dirt. At one point, about 100 yards from the road, it looked as if someone had made a rather large model of a foot and had stamped a few impressions in the dirt. Although they were not perfectly clear, it was readily evident that our "Monster" walked on only one foot—his right foot. And, certainly for all of the accounts describing "Gooney" as anywhere from 7 feet to 10 feet in height, he did not leave a very deep impression in the dirt. So, he was either very light on his feet, or very, very skinny. I picked up a tree branch and erased the marks before leaving, hoping to cut off some of the tales that would have surely sprouted from the dress and footprints. Still, the stories grew and circulated with the passing days, weeks and months. It seemed that nothing was going to chase away Howard County's Gooney Monster.

Months passed and the calls continued to light up the police switchboard, but not as frequently. Then on a very warm Monday evening, the police dispatcher called and told me that Trooper First Class Pete Edge of the Maryland State Police asked that I meet him at Kindler Road and Route 32 regarding "The Gooney Monster."

Pete said, "About an hour ago I took a report from a young woman who said she was driving on Murray Hill Road, when this very large, horrible looking creature stepped out in front of her car. Jimmy, this girl was terrified. I've never seen anything like it. She was shaking and crying and had a very hard time telling me what happened. She couldn't give much in the way of a description, other than it was big and horrible looking, and ran off into the woods."

We talked about the sightings of this alleged monster and

wondered if someone was foolish enough to be running around in a costume to keep the story going. We agreed that, if this was the case, it was a very foolish prank, because some of the people flocking to the area were still carrying guns.

When the shift ended, I went to Buell's Restaurant for a sandwich and a beer, and found fellow Howard County Police Officers Griff Jones, Denny Laumann and Karl Beazley already there. When I sat down with them, Denny said, "Everything quiet this evening?"

"No," I said, and proceeded to tell them about my chat with Pete Edge.

Denny jumped to his feet and said, "That's it. We're going down there right now and find this thing."

"Laumann, you're outta your damn mind," Griff shot back. "I ain't going down there and look for some monster. I believe these things exist and I'm not goin'."

While the argument between Griff and Denny continued, I smiled and thought how comical this had to look to others listening to the verbal joust.

Griff was truly a bear of a man, standing about 5'10" and weighing in at least 245 pounds. He was an all down home country born and raised farm boy, and as strong as an ox. Yet, here he was confessing his belief in, and fears of "monsters."

Denny, on the other hand, was 6'5" tall and tipped the scales at around 220 pounds and was willing to lead a search party to find the beast.

Karl was probably just about six feet tall, but was slender in build and the wide receiver on the department's flag football team.

As a last resort, Griff said his wife was expecting him home before midnight, and that's why he couldn't go off searching for Big Foot.

In no time at all, Denny had Griff in the phone booth, calling his wife. His first words, "Betty, I know you're not gonna believe this…" That's when Denny grabbed the phone from Griff and told

Betty that he was leading a Safari of "Great White Hunters" out to search for The Gooney Monster. Besides, he had elected Griff as the driver for this excursion into the unknown.

By the time we reached Griff's car, I was beginning to question my sanity as well as their mental state, or at least Denny's. But, there we were with two six packs of National Boh, climbing into Griff's two-tone green, 1956 Ford, setting out in search of Sasquatch, or whatever it was lurking in the fields and forests between Murray Hill and Kindler Roads. Of course, we had to stop and put two dollars worth of gas in the car before our "fearless" outing began in earnest.

Karl and I sat in the back seat, sipping a beer, while Griff continued to argue with Denny over the merits of this night time search. His plea to wait until daylight, when the sunshine would provide better lighting conditions by which to search, didn't sway Denny's lust for adventure.

We made it to Murray Hill Road and I directed them to the bridge, where we pulled over and stopped.

"Laumann, I don't like this one damn bit," Griff said. "I wanna get outta here and go home."

"Griff, we're gonna look for this thing right now. Stop the car and let's go."

"Laumann, you're outta your goddamn mind. I ain't gettin' outta my car and I'm sure as hell not gonna go runnin' around in the woods. Jesus, look how dark it is."

He was certainly right about it being dark. Towering Oak and various other trees, which almost completely blocked out the starlight, surrounded the area. And, it was a moonless night.

But, a minute later he was walking behind me, down the embankment toward the streambed, while Denny took the lead of this hunting party. And, as far as the hunting party description, I was the only one carrying a firearm and a flashlight. I had a five shot, Smith and Wesson, snubbed nosed revolver, which I doubt would have done any more than piss off this beast if it decided to kick the snot out of us and send us home.

5

"Jimmy, can I carry the gun?" Griff whispered.

"No, Griff, I've only had one beer."

"Let me hold the flashlight."

Trying not to laugh, I said, "I need the light to see if this thing attacks us."

"Jimmy, don't say shit like that. I don't like this. I don't like being here. I should be home in bed, not out here in the woods with that crazy ass Laumann lookin' for some damn monster."

Twenty minutes of stomping around the streambed finally convinced Denny that the monster wasn't there. So, there we were, back in the car, with "Maharishi" Laumann directing Griff to the next search area.

In no time at all, he was directing Griff to turn off Murray Hill Road and on to what was a private driveway. This was certainly no ordinary driveway. As was the case with the main road, trees line both sides of the drive, but the branches reached out from both sides, intertwining in places, making it seem as if we were entering a very dark cave.

The heavy underbrush, consisting of grass, honeysuckle, weeds and briars also lined the driveway, adding to the darkness.

"Stop the car," Laumann said. Reluctantly, Griff braked to a stop. "Okay, cut the engine and roll the windows down."

"What!" Griff screamed. "Now, I know you're' crazy. I'm not turning the engine off. What if this thing comes out and the car won't start?"

Denny tried to reach across Griff and grab the keys. From where Karl and I sat, the wrestling match taking place in the front seat was very funny. Tall and lanky, fighting Grizzly Griff for the car keys. After a brief struggle, Laumann got his wish and Griff cut the engine.

When he rolled the window down, Griff said, "Put that damn window up. What if it jumps in the car with us."

"It won't jump in the car."

"Laumann, I don't like this. I told you, I believe in these things and I don't wanna stay here."

"Shhhhh. Just open your window and listen."

"I'm not opening my damn window. I wanna get outta here."

Night time in a place such as we were, is anything but quiet. Nocturnal birds and animals prowl in the darkness in search of food. So, there were the normal sounds in the thicket of some of those creatures moving about, which gave Griff's already shattered nerves another jolt. Then an owl screeched.

"Holy shit! Let's get outta here."

Over Denny's objections, Griff had the car back out on Murray Hill Road in no time. But, the hunt was still on. With our fearless leader directing, Griff turned from Murray Hill Road on to Vollmerhausen Road, which was another tree lined, very dark road.

Of course, after the owl incident, Griff was in a greater than ever hurry to end his brief career as a monster hunter. While Denny watched and listened, he spouted reason after reason why we should just go home. He was adamantly voicing his objections to going on with the hunt as we neared the crest of a hill. Suddenly, something darted from a clearing on our right, into the road, and vanished over the top of the hill. And, whatever it was, it was rather large.

"Oh, Jesus Christ! What the hell was that?" Griff screamed and slammed on the brakes.

"Go after it! Go after it! Denny yelled, lunging across the seat and stomping down on the accelerator. "Go, go! Chase it."

"I'm not gonna chase it."

They were seated side by side, fighting for control of the car. Screaming and yelling, the battle for control went on, until Griff's foot slipped off the brake and we shot up and over the peak of the hill. Griff screamed, as the large animal suddenly appeared in front us, trotting down Vollmerhausen Road, as though it didn't have a care in the world and, by all appearances, following the double yellow line.

"Damn," Denny blurted. "It's a jackass."

I laughed. "Yeah. Now, there are five of us out here."

With nothing, but another jackass to boast of for our efforts into the world of monster hunting, our Safari came to an end. But, calls reporting sightings of "The Gooney Monster" continued. At least one call a week kept the tale alive, and the curious and the sceptical arrived on Friday and Saturday evenings, hoping to catch a glimpse of whatever it was lurking in the darkness.

Months passed, and Police Officer Joe Collins was patrolling Mayfield Avenue in Elkridge on a cloudy afternoon, when nature called. He pulled off on the dirt drive leading to the Rod and Gun Club and travelled a "safe" distance to answer the call.

"I was about to take care of the business at hand when I happened to glance up into the trees. Jesus! There was this thing up in the trees looking down at me. At that instant I no longer had to worry about nature's call. It took a few seconds to see that whatever it was, wasn't real, or at least alive.

"The creature had been tied up in the trees and at an angle, so it would appear to be looking down on anyone who drove or walked along the dirt road. It was at least 10 feet or more in height, and its center width was probably four feet or better. The head was very large, with wild looking eyes and very long, pointed teeth. Attached to one hand by string or wire was a huge bone.

"I called Wayne Ridgely, who was the area supervisor that day and asked him to meet me."

When he arrived and saw the thing, he said, "Okay, we need pictures."

"After a dozen or so photographs were taken, he decided that we had to transport it to the police station. Well, it certainly wasn't going to fit in the backseat of the police car. So, Howard County Public Works sent a dump truck, which was the only thing large enough to hall this beast."

At Howard County Police Headquarters there was no place to store it. A decision was made to stand it in the back corner of the fence behind the police station. It was tied and anchored to the fence, and more photos were taken. The pictures were taken with

Detective Lee Hajek and Officer Wayne Ridgely standing beside it to show its gigantic size.

Next, the local news media was notified and arrived to "get the big story" on the apprehension of the monster. Although this elaborately constructed beast was not found anywhere near Murray Hill and Kindler Roads, newspaper headlines boldly proclaimed **"Gooney Monster Captured."** But, the accompanying story, and photographs, brought a sudden end to the sightings and weekend searches for the legendary creature. He vanished with the evening sunset, never to be heard from again.

It's a Jungle in There

Harry Wink, Joseph Ganascioli, Leo Cordero and a cast of unidentified friends

Police Officers Harry Wink, Joe Ganascioli, and Leo Cordero reported finding a door open, night after night, on the same three-story office building, located near Lake Kittamaqundi in Columbia, Md. They soon grew weary of having to search the building, top to bottom, and checking each office space to be certain no businesses had been burglarized. The building housed The Library Disco, as well as dozens of other businesses, and Harry and Joe noted that the front doors were often found standing wide open.

On one occasion, not only the front doors allowing access to the building were open, but also the doors permitting entry to the disco were standing open. A search of the club, showed cases of expensive wines and champagne stacked near a door, which if opened, would have allowed a thief to carry them away undetected.

"Shopping made easy for every thief in the county," Harry muttered. "Then we'd get the blame if the place got cleaned out."

Calls in the wee hours of the morning, to various business

owners, asking them to meet officers at the building to determine if anything was amiss, always seemed to bring out a very blunt and sometimes obscenity laced refusal. Follow-up action during normal business hours also failed to identify anyone who wanted to accept responsibility for insuring security of the building. However, one owner suggested that when the building was found to be unlocked, that the police assign an officer to standby there for the remainder of the night to guard the building. The response to his suggestion was as blunt as the late night retorts given to police.

Not long after the disco was found open, officers stopped calling the dispatchers and reporting the doors not properly secured, and they did not report checking the offices for burglaries. The building was still left unlocked, or doors were found propped open, but it seemed Harry and Joe and few friends found a way to fight back.

Business owners and employees arriving for work, walked into the lobby, pressed the button and waited patiently for the elevator. Imagine their surprise when the doors opened and they discovered every potted plant from the building stuffed into the elevator.

These were not small plants and pots by any means and, in some cases, required two or more people to move them. But, as strange as it may seem, no one called the police and reported the prank. Yet, the plants in the elevator didn't serve as a warning to those who were careless enough to leave the building open after working hours.

Then one night it happened. Harry and Joe found an office space open on the third floor. Harry spoke a coded message over the radio and help was on the way. In no time at all, file cabinets, tables, chairs and lamps were being moved out of the office by police wearing gloves. Family photographs and individual pictures of wives, husbands, pets and children were the last items taken.

The first arrivals not only discovered their office space partially empty, but also quickly found that the restrooms had been converted to makeshift offices. Photographs were displayed on the tops of urinals, and the backs of commodes. Chairs, tables and lamps and been arranged in neat exhibits, while file cabinets were stored inside restroom stalls.

Still, there were no calls to police reporting the "office relocation" project. But, it was noted by officers patrolling that particular beat that the building was not left open as frequently.

Sunday Morning Seasick Blues

Primary Performing Star: PFC Joseph P. Ganascioli

"God, I should know better than to go out partying the night before a dayshift, even if the shift was a Sunday." Words spoken by Officer Joseph Ganascioli when he arrived for work.

I went right to Sergeant Lilley and begged and pleaded for mercy. "Sarge, please let me work Sector Five instead of Sector Eight."

He stared at me for what felt like minutes, but I know it was only a few seconds. He smiled and said, "Joe, I know how you feel. Sure as hell, a lot of us have been there at one time or another, but we took our lumps and worked our area." At that point I was sure he was going to say "no, you work Sector Eight." Instead he laughed. "Okay, Joe, you can work Sector Five. Just remember, you handle any and all calls in that area."

"Yes, sir," I said, feeling as if I'd just won the lottery. Hell, Sector Five is never busy on a Sunday. I was home free.

"When I left the building to go to my patrol car, I was really miserable. It was already hot and I knew it was only going to get hotter as the day went on. My head, which was already pounding, felt like it was about to explode and, naturally, the brutal heat wasn't helping. God, how I wished it was winter. At least the cold weather would make me feel a little better. And then there was my stomach. Jesus, the ride into work made me queasy, and the very thought of trying to eat made me nauseous. I just wanted to go somewhere and hide, and pray for the day to end quickly so I could go home and pass out. But, 1700 hours already felt like it was months away. Still, I had the comfort of working Sector Five.

"Although I turned down the radio, every time a call was dispatched, I groaned. The dispatcher's voice seemed like it was screaming in my ear, making my head throb even more. And, my stomach—oh, a churning mass of acid and surely some remnants of last night's excesses, making me wish I could puke. I could only ask myself, 'Why did I do it?'

"Then, somewhere between 10:00 and 10:15, that irritating, nagging voice was calling my number. Oh, God, please let this be a mistake, I moaned as I reached for my radio. A moment later the dispatcher was telling me to go to the reservoir to meet Fire and Rescue Personnel regarding a body in the water. She proceeded to refresh my aching memory, telling me the body was possibly that of a man who had gone fishing over a week ago and failed to return home. No! This can't be happening. Not the way I feel.

"I drove to the reservoir and found Fire and Rescue members waiting patiently for me. The instant I stepped out of my car they had to be thinking that I looked as bad as the body we were about to go looking for. I saw a few knowing smiles as I walked toward them and I began to pray that this was all a joke. But, one of them told me I would have to accompany them on the boat while they retrieved the body and, suddenly, I realized my day was going from bad to worse.

"Everybody working the shift knew of my over indulgence the night before. I had already taken a beating from my 'good friends' before we left the briefing room only a few hours ago. I knew that at this very moment, they had to be laughing their asses off over my situation and the morning beating would only pale in comparison to what was ahead.

"I hoped for a last minute reprieve when Sergeant Lilley and Officer Leo Cordero arrived. When I asked Sergeant Lilley if there was any way I could escape this call he laughed."

"Sorry, Joe, it's your sector. Officer Cordero is more than capable of securing the roadway and keeping the curiosity seekers out of the area. Besides, a nice ride in the boat might be just what you need. The hot sun beating down on you, while the boat rocks up and down and the breeze in your face."

"If I thought I could have gotten away with calling him a no good prick, I would have. But, I didn't want my ass kicked in front of all the firemen, so I climbed into the boat and sat up front.

"The instant the boat pulled away from shore, I knew my day was going right to hell. If this body was the man who vanished over a week ago, it had to be in bad shape.

"Hot weather and in the water made for a bad combination. In a matter of minutes my nightmare became reality, it was the missing man.

"For a little while everything was a blur. Then, there I was, sitting in the boat, almost on top of a decomposing body and, to be honest, I can't find the words to describe what it was like. The boat was headed back to shore and I swear the prick driving was going as slow as he possibly could. The shoreline looked like it was 20 miles away, and my condition was reaching the point where I was certain I might be in need of last rites.

"Finally we reached shore and I hurried out of the boat, praying for my queasy stomach to settle before I puked all over myself. Dry land seemed to help ease my urge to barf, but Sergeant Lilley had one more "minor" chore for me to perform. He told me to check the body of the deceased for identification.

"Reluctantly—very reluctantly actually, I leaned over the body and reached for a pocket. The instant I touched the corpse, air and gas belched into my face and I was running for the nearest bush. In seconds, insult piled high on last night's self-inflicted "injuries" as I puked all over bushes, ants, leaves, crawling insects and my shoes. And, at that moment of adding insult to injury, I Joseph P. Ganascioli, learned a lesson never to be forgotten. When you come to work, be prepared to work."

Life and Times with the Maryland State Police

With First Sergeant Peter Fairchild Edge in the lead role, assisted by a cast of fellow Maryland State Troopers and other friends.

Caught in the Act

It was a Sunday afternoon, it was hot as hell and back in "the good old days" we didn't have air conditioning in our cars. And here I am riding around Laurel, with all the windows open, hoping for a breeze of any kind to cool my sweaty ass off. I was sure that all of my friends, at least the few sane ones I had, were at the beach, drinking beer and laughing at me for working.

I wasn't too far from the hospital when I heard what sounded like screams and, at first, I thought it just a bird or some other animal squawking about the heat. But then, I very clearly heard someone screaming "Rape." Well, the heat be damned. I was a Trooper on a mission to find a crime in progress, because it always seemed we got to a crime after the fact.

It didn't take too long to find this little park area where the screams where coming from, and a second later I saw a man holding a woman down on the ground. I stopped my cruiser, jumped out and started running toward the couple. The woman was really putting up a fight and screaming rape and, by now, my adrenaline was pumping like crazy. I pulled my "slapjack" out of my pocket— which is what we carried in those days. It was flat and one end was filled with lead. In a few steps I was beside them. I didn't say a word. I just raised the slapjack and swung for the fence. I caught the guy on the left side of his head and the shot didn't just open a gash, it peeled skin and flesh down into a roll that looked like a canapé. And, blood was everywhere. He fell off of the woman and rolled to the ground, unconscious.

That's when I noticed that the woman had blood all over her. After a few seconds I was aware that all of that blood wasn't from the guy I had just cold-cocked. It looked like she had cut marks on her wrists and they were bleeding. The next thing I know, the man I had smacked was trying to push himself up and get to his feet. He looked at me and said, "I know what this looks like, and I don't know if you're gonna believe me or not, but she's my girlfriend and she's suicidal. I was trying to stop her from killing herself."

Well, I just kinda stared at him and thought, *Well, Peter, if it's possible for a Maryland State Trooper to be transferred to Siberia, that's where your ass is going.*

Things got a little hazy at this point because I thought I was charging into a crime in progress and was going to save the day. But, before I knew it we were at the hospital and he was being taken care of and the doctors and nurses were trying to calm her down.

They managed to get her calmed down long enough to clean her wounds—her self-inflicted wounds, and stitch 'em up. But, the first chance she got, she ripped all the stitches out with her teeth.

Of course, all the while I'm imagining the things that are gonna happen to me for smacking this poor guy. I was just picturing myself in front of a firing squad when the guy walks over and says, "Hey, everything's fine. I know what you must've thought and there's no hard feelings. You were just doing your job." But, I don't see something like that happening in today's society.

Up on the Rooftop

Back in my early days it felt like there was so much territory to cover and it seemed I was always at the other end when something happened. So, here I am in Ellicott City when I get a call to back up another trooper on a possible burglary in progress. He's in some place called Taneytown, which I have no idea where that might be, other than it's got to be over 19,000 miles away. Anyway, I started driving in a westerly direction after looking at my map and hoping I could make it by the end of the week.

Every now and then Corporal Bill Brooks would ask me where I was and I had to get on the radio and pretend I knew. But, after what felt like 37 hours of driving, I finally found this building in Taneytown and there was a trooper outside. This had to be the right place.

I got out of my car after turning on my radio's outside speaker, because back in those days there was no such thing as a hand held radio. I walked over to this trooper, who I later found out was Donny Newcomer and he just grins and says, "Hi, Hummer."

I ignored the Hummer comment and said, "What's the problem?"

"Heard a noise up there." He pointed to the rooftop of the building. "You go up there and check it out, Hummer."

Okay, I'm still the rookie around town and the next thing I know I'm climbing up this ladder, heading for the roof. I finally made it to the rooftop and started searching for any signs of a burglar or a burglary. After a few minutes, I hadn't located a burglar or signs of forced entry into the building, so I walked back to the edge of the roof. I looked down and saw Donny in his car and he was grinning from ear to ear.

"See ya, Hummer," he yelled. Then he drove off, laughing.

I wondered what was so damn funny and then I noticed the ladder was missing.

I hurried to the edge of the roof and there it was. That damn miserable prick had taken it down and laid it on the parking lot. I started yelling for him to come back and get me off the roof and, at the same time, I can hear Brooks calling me on the radio asking how much longer I'm gonna be tied up.

After a few minutes of waiting, I realized that that no good shit, Don Newcomer, wasn't gonna return and get me off the roof. I knew there were no open trap doors or any other way for me to easily escape from my rooftop jail. So, I decided to take the next best way out and slide down the drain spout.

Those were the days when I was in great physical condition. Well, better shape than I'm in now. Anyway, here I am wearing a gun belt and all accessories, easing my ass over the side of the building and calling Newcomer every no good prick in the book. I managed to get over the side without falling and I was sure that was in my favor. I was working my way down the drain spout, realizing that I wasn't Batman or Spiderman, when I felt the spout move. Oh, shit!

So, now in panic mode, I tried to hurry down, but the drain spout was really starting to pull away from the side of the building. A few seconds later I was playing paratrooper, without a parachute and hit the ground, landing on my back. Of course, the fall knocked the wind out of me and, I was lying there on the ground gasping and groaning, promising myself that I would shoot Newcomer the next time I saw him—if I ever saw the miserable shit again.

In the meantime, Bill Brooks is still calling me on the radio, sounding more and more pissed off with each call. Somehow I made it to my car and then just played with the radio, mumbling, gasping and rubbing the mic on my pant leg, hoping that Brooks would just forget me.

A few weeks later, I attended a mandatory troopers meeting and, wouldn't you know it, Donny Newcomer was there. He walked right over to me, still grinning from that prank he'd pulled and said, "Hi ya, Hummer."

I laughed instead of shooting him and, in no time at all, Donny and I were the best of friends. Although, I'm not sure I've ever forgiven him for abandoning me on the roof.

Citizen's Complaint

Trooper Bobby Whacker had made a traffic stop on 295 and it wasn't long before he was on the radio, asking me to meet him at the location of his stop. In a few minutes, he was telling me that the driver of the car demanded to see his supervisor. Well, I certainly wasn't a supervisor and, in fact, I was still a slick sleeve, but what the hell, I thought I'd do my best on the spur of the moment.

This was the same time that Bobby and I had talked about doing something funny.

Not just a little funny, but outrageously funny. This seemed like it was the appropriate time to do it.

I approached the car, noticing that it had California tags and knew this would be interesting. I identified myself, being sure to mumble my name, and asked the driver what the problem was.

"I don't think your trooper's very professional," he said. "I think he was too blunt in asking for my driver's license and he could've been much clearer in his explanation for stopping me."

I nodded. "Sir, may I have your driver's license." He didn't say anything. He just handed me his license and stared at me.

Remember this was back in the days of the old paper driver's licenses. The days when it was easy to alter the license and they practically wore out from being carried in your wallet. Well, after I took his license I didn't say a word. I pulled a small container of peanut butter out of my pocket, along with a little plastic knife and spread the peanut butter all over his license. The guy just gave me a blank stare when I took a bite out of his license, chewed it up and swallowed it.

Bobby burst into a fit of laughter when I started to eat the license and by now the driver's completely dumbfounded. Bobby's doubled over holding his sides, gasping for air and finally he fell down on the ground behind the guy's car. I kept gnawing on the license until it was gone and then I calmly walked back to my car. At which time I jumped in and sped off at 23,000 miles an hour, hoping the guy didn't get my car number.

Of course, I left poor Bobby lying there behind the guy's car, still laughing. I don't know how long the guy stayed there, but he must have gotten tired of waiting for somebody to come back and he eventually just drove off.

I talked with Bobby later and he asked what I'd do if the guy actually showed up for court, because he had written him a summons before he called me. I told him I didn't think the guy would show up, because he certainly wasn't gonna drive back to Maryland to stand trial for a traffic ticket. Even if he returned to stand trial, I was sure Judge Clark would never believe him if he told him I ate his license. Of course, if he did say that I ate his license and Judge Clark asked, I would hafta admit it and take the consequences. But the guy never did show up for trial.

Victim of the Snake

As a young trooper I had heard many stories about Robert "Snake" Long, but had not had the pleasure of meeting the legendary prankster. But, the day came when I was sitting in the Trooper's Room, where all our cubbyholes are located, and a TFC walked in and went straight to his cubby to get his mail. That's when I realized that he was the one and only "Snake" Long. He looked over at me and said, "Hi, little fella. Hi, little fella."

I said hello and tried to pretend I wasn't staring at him.

I had heard so many stories about this man and his crazy sense of humor, but I guess I wasn't completely convinced that he was really that wild. I sat there quietly watching, while he opened one of the envelopes he'd taken out of his mailbox. He took the letter out and began reading.

I almost fell out of my chair when he started talking to the letter. He'd read a sentence out loud and then talk back to the letter, giving some rude, lewd or otherwise smart assed reply. I was trying not to laugh out loud, because I wasn't sure how'd he take it, but I couldn't help it. Every time he opened another letter, he would talk to it, like the person who wrote it was standing there in front of him. Now, I was howling, but I couldn't help it. "Snake" was reading these letters and talking to them as if I wasn't even there. When he finished with the last letter, he looked over at me. "You okay, little fella. You okay, little fella."

I squeaked out a weak, "Yes, sir" and was happy that I didn't piss myself in front of him.

I guess it was about a week later when I was working the

night shift and "Snake" was my partner on Route One. About an hour into the shift he called and told me the car in front of me didn't have a front tag and that I should stop it and take appropriate action.

In those "old days" we had a light on the right front fender which, when lighted, read, "Stop, Police." It was positioned on the fender in such a way so as to shine into the face of the driver of the car we wanted to stop. Well, I made damn sure I was going to do everything right on this stop, because I had to impress "Snake." I had my hat on when I pulled along side the car and turned on the overhead light and, next, I looked directly at the driver when I flipped the switch on the fender light.

His head spun and he looked right at me with this dumb look on his face, but he kept driving. I flipped the switch off and back on again and, once more, this guy gave me this dumb ass look and kept driving. Here we are, headed northbound on Route One and the driver is refusing to stop. So much for impressing "Snake."

I kept flipping the switch for the fender light off and on, but the guy wouldn't obey the signals. I called over the radio that the driver was refusing to pull over and that's when "Snake" told me to forget the stop and return to the barrack. I couldn't understand why he called off the stop, especially since he ordered me to make it in the first place. But, he was giving the orders.

I should have known when I pulled on to the lot at Waterloo that something was very wrong, because "Snake" and a few other troopers were waiting when I arrived. I got out of my car and right away "Snake" says, "Did you inspect your car before you went on the road?"

Of course, I inspected my car, you dipshit. That's standard procedure before every shift, I thought, but certainly didn't say it. Instead I said, "Oh, yes, sir. I inspect my car at the beginning of every tour."

"Well, maybe you should inspect it again. Turn on all the lights, you know, check everything."

That still wasn't a clue, but I did as I was told. I started walking around the car and everything looked just fine. That is until I took a second look at my fender light. Oh, shit! Somebody had

---

---

removed the original cover from the light and replaced it. My light no longer said, "Stop, Police" it very clearly read "Fuck You."

Jesus Christ! That's what I'd been flashing at the guy and that's why he didn't stop.

By now, "Snake" and everybody else was howling and I knew I had fallen victim to one of his demented jokes. Naturally, it was my ass that was gonna get in hot—no probably boiling water when the guy complained. But, for reasons I'll never know or even understand, the guy never complained. Well, maybe he thought that every last one of us was insane and it was better to make believe it never happened.

You Should Know

After graduating from the State Police Academy, I was assigned to ride with John Himmelman as part of field training. John was a great guy and a stickler for making sure the job was done right. He questioned me on procedures, motor vehicle and criminal law, and rules and regulations. John was also one of those troopers who had a sharp eye and keen awareness of anything and everything going on around him. He could spot a violation across four lanes of highway and quote the article or code number and section for the infraction. Unfortunately, he expected me to be the same way.

During one of our shifts he suddenly turned to me and said, "Stop that car now," pointing to the one directly in front of us.

Without hesitation I activated the overhead light and pulled the car over. Then I looked over at John and said, "Why did I stop this guy?"

He just looked at me. "You should know."

Well, Jesus, I didn't have a clue as to why I pulled the guy over. I started walking up to the car, hoping to see something wrong with the tag or taillights, but I wasn't that lucky. I couldn't see a thing. The next thing I knew, I was standing beside the car and wondering what I was going to do. I asked for the man's drivers license and registration and kept trying to think of a violation of any kind, but drew a blank.

The man looked up at me and said, "Why'd you stop me?"

"You should know," I replied, figuring that if John could be a smart-ass with me, I could be the same with this guy.

Before I knew what was happening, he started rattling off a half dozen reasons why I could've pulled him over. I nodded. "Yes, sir, that's right. But I'm only gonna write you a warning this time."

I walked back to the cruiser and wrote out a warning for a speed violation. A few seconds later I gave the paper to the man and sent him on his way happy as hell with a warning.

When I got back in the cruiser, John said, "Why'd you write him a warning?"

I just couldn't help myself. I smiled and said, "You should know."

Damn, John didn't think that was funny at all. In fact, he was positively pissed off over my response. So pissed off, actually, that he didn't speak to me for a week. Yet, it didn't keep John and I from eventually becoming very good friends

West Virginia Coal Dust

I'd say working the coalmine detail was probably one I truly enjoyed. I had Terry Katz with me and we headed out to West "By God" Virginia because of the feud between union and non-union coal mine workers. The feud started when the unionized workers in the West Virginia mines went on strike and the non-union workers at the Mitiki mine in Western Maryland continued to work. Well, the good ole West Virginia boys decided they would just drop by from time to time and toss some dynamite into the Mitiki mine and shut it down. And, Terry and I had to make sure that didn't happen.

We rolled into a small West Virginia town somewhere after 5:00 AM and the next thing I know, I'm being pulled over by the local police officer. He walks over to the car and says, "You were doin' 25 in 35 zone, and I'm gonna write you a ticket."

"But, I'm drivin' 10 miles under the posted speed limit."

"Speed limit's 35 and I'm writin' you a ticket," he said. "You were doin' 25 and if you don't believe me, look at my grand pappy. He's got the radar gun."

I walked over to his car and I couldn't believe it. There was grand pappy all right, sittin' in the car in his bathrobe, an orange drink in one hand and holding the radar gun in the other! "Look," I said. "The radar says 25 and that's under the speed limit."

"Don't you know better than to argue with the police," he said, and went right on and wrote me a ticket.

I signed the ticket, which gave me and Terry great cover for the assignment, because he pulled us over in front of the local bar and restaurant. Of course, it was already open and we went inside, where we got a warm greeting from all the locals.

"That son-of-a-bitch got you too, huh?" one of them said.

I laughed. "Sure did."

"Well, we'll pay him back for ya later on."

I didn't pay too much attention to that comment, because I was really caught up by the breakfast one of the coal miners was eating. It was certainly a first—at least for me. He had a chew of tobacco stuck in his jaw, another stuck under his lip and he was smokin' a Pall Mall. He had a coffee, a double shot of Jack Daniels, a Beer and this was 5:30 in the morning. He's got all this in front of him, chewin' Copenhagen and eatin' a bacon and egg sandwich. Well, I couldn't help but see that he hadn't spit and I just had to say something.

"Excuse me, sir."

"Yeah."

"I noticed you haven't spit."

He just gave me a look. "A real man don't spit, boy."

I didn't puke, but I said, "Well, hell, shake hands with a little girl." I mean I'd already been outside nine times to spit, while just tryin' to keep up with him. So, here I was tryin' to put on my best "hard-ass" front, but I couldn't match this guy.

He stuck his hand out to shake hands with me, and it's all covered in coal dust. I mean ground in, lifetime coal dust, but I shook his hand.

On our way up, I kept seein' these signs that said Ramp. I always thought a ramp was something you used to put your boat in the water, but I didn't see any water. So, I thought I'd ask this old guy what all these signs meant.

"Sir, can you tell me what Ramp is?"

He gives me that look again. "You ain't from these parts is ya?"

"No, sir."

Then he explains that Ramp is a West Virginia onion that grows wild and it's part onion and part garlic. "Yeah, boy, it's a wild ass onion that Harry Truman liked. Every year we have a Harry Truman Ramp day here."

Later on I found out these things are really good and they are positively great with Hamburgers.

By the end of the day, Terry and I knew a few of the boys and pretty soon we were invited to their meetings. We'd find out when they were going over to the "other side of the border" to attack the mine, and they'd always find the Maryland State Police TAC Team waiting for them. They could never figure out why they had such a streak of bad luck.

On the funny side, they did keep their word about paying the cop back who wrote me the ticket. A group of them went to his house late on the night he stopped me and turned his car over on its roof. The light bar broke off and all the oil ran out of the engine as a result of their prank, but that didn't keep "Deputy Dick" from doing his duty. He and grand pappy just got a bunch of their friends to flip the car back on its wheels and put oil in the engine. In no time at all, he was back out there nailing them "speeders."

Cat for a Hat

I was sent into Baltimore City to set up a heroin deal and found that my initial contact was a guy who worked in a gay bar. Of course, back in those days, these guys were not out in the streets holding hands and screaming for a marriage license. They were still very much hidden in the background.

26

Anyway, I met this guy and while I was waiting for him to arrange the deal, a very lovely woman walks in. I was a young, handsome "stud-muffin" back then and she invited me upstairs. Well, my contact says go ahead and I thought I was going upstairs to make a heroin buy.

While I was walking up the stairs behind her, I started wondering if she was really a she. But, it didn't really make any difference, I was there to buy dope, not get involved with some streetwalker. When we got to her room, she had other ideas and started taking her clothes off. I still wasn't certain what this street creature was, but when she finally got out of her clothes she did appear to be authentic. Then, it went downhill.

She was peddling pussy and I was looking for heroin. I started making excuses why I didn't want to partake of the goods being offered and backed out of the room. She took offense and started throwing everything she could get her hands on at me— shoes, cups, glasses and I think the toaster went by.

I kept retreating and felt something land on my head. At first I wasn't sure what it was and then I felt this stinging sensation. I thought she might have thrown acid at me and then I felt the pain increase. There was this loud, "Meeeoooowwwww, fsssst, fsssst, meeeoooowwwww" and I realized I had a damn cat on top of my head. I grabbed it and started pulling, but the goddamn thing had its claws imbedded in my scalp. Down the stairs and out the door I went with this cat still attached to my skull. I don't know how long it took me to get it off my head, but I can only imagine what the sight must have looked like. Me yelling, tugging and pulling while the cat howled and hissed.

Somehow, I was still able to hook up with the dope dealer, but he would only sell me a very small quantity. But I think my unscheduled meeting with the pussy peddler and my battle with the mountain lion she dropped on my head ended any chances for a major score. On the bright side, I didn't come down with rabies or crotch cooties.

Victimized by the County Police

In the early days of my career there was always a good relationship between the State Police and Howard County Police.

We were always there, watching out for each other and, as those friendships formed the door opened for a battle of practical jokes and pranks of imaginative proportions.

I must have had a sign hanging on my ass that said, "Get this guy. He's easy." I fell victim to more than my share of jokes over the years, especially to one smart-assed county officer, who shall remain nameless. Although I will tell you, he's the author of this book.

I'm not certain when I was first victimized by this demented pervert, or how many times I've fallen prey to his always scheming mind, but in the 40 plus years that I've known him, believe me, it's a lot. I've been called by Weight Watchers, Jenny Craig, Fat Boys Anonymous (if there is such a thing), women who call saying they have the hots for me, and then burst into fits of laughter after they ask if I really weigh 980 pounds.

There was a bumper sticker on my unmarked police car that said "Wine Me, Dine me, Sixty-nine me" and I drove around with it for over a week before it was pointed out to me. So much for my fantastic powers of observation, right? When I finally caught up to him and "thanked" him for it, he immediately offered to replace it with one he just happened to have on hand. So, for the next week, I carefully circled my car, each and every time before I drove it, just to be certain that I wasn't displaying a fancy blue and silver bumper sticking reading, "Save a Mouse. Eat a Pussy."

If there is such a thing as a crowning gem in his factory of pranks, it's probably the letter he sent to me at the Waterloo Barrack. Of course, I was away on a skiing trip at the time and he called the barrack to be certain he had the correct address. Well, I think his call to the barrack really had a twofold purpose. First, to be sure of the address and second, to alert everyone that something was headed my way in the mail.

When I returned to work, everybody seemed almost too happy to see me. But, I passed it off until I reached my desk. That's when I noticed the bright blue envelope, which had been carefully placed in the center of my desk. The color made it impossible to miss, but even more eye catching were the bold letters splashed across the envelope.

LAST CHANCE DATING SERVICE – APPLICATION REJECTED

I probably should've just torn the thing up then and there and tossed it in the trash or run it through the shredder. But, no I had to open it and see what it said. In a nutshell (the letter was almost four damn pages long) it said they were more than happy to reject my application for a date, because no woman in her right mind would date a guy who had a scorched Brillo Pad for hair and weighed a ton.

It went on to say the State of Maryland was going bankrupt just buying shock absorbers for my car and uniforms that had to be made out of a circus tent. And then there was the part saying that Peterbilt and Kenworth couldn't even build a tractor large enough to haul my wide ass around. Of course, there was a very kind segment at the end telling me to contact Car and Driver Magazine because they might be able to set up a date for me with a 1949 Hudson Hornet.

Well, I foolishly left the letter on my desk while I prowled around the barrack in a huff, blaming my ex-wife for having a hand in it. Naturally, my "friends" couldn't resist the temptation provided and they faxed a copy of the letter to every State Police Barrack in the state. In no time at all, I was receiving calls, cards and faxes offering suggestions on dating, dieting, car maintenance and uniform care. Okay, it was my fault for leaving the letter on my desk.

I just couldn't get the idea out of my head that my ex-wife wrote the letter, or had somehow played a part in whole scheme. That is until my "dear friend, Jimmy" stopped by the barrack one evening "just to see how I was doing."

It was about a month after I received the letter and we just shot the breeze for about 20 minutes. He was on his way out the door when he turned around and said, "Hey, Pete, did you ever get that date?"

I know I must have looked stupid, but I walked right into it. "Date? What date?"

"The one with the '49 Hudson."

Son-of-a-bitch! The light went on bright and clear. I had been victimized once more by this evil-minded joker. I should've known from the beginning that it was him and I don't know why I didn't suspect him immediately. But, at the time my first, and only, suspect was my ex-wife.

Bright Lights

Our State Police cars didn't have spotlights like the county cars and, at times, it was inconvenient as hell, if not hazardous to our health. One of the troopers at the Waterloo Barrack, Trooper Carr, decided to remedy the situation and went out and bought some landing lights. He said these were great, because they could be hooked up in the grill in place or our bright lights or high beam lights.

I had a set installed on my white Plymouth—you know the unmarked car I had with the Port-a-wall White Wall Tires. The White Walls they blew off when you drove over 30 miles an hour. Anyway, I couldn't wait for my first opportunity to try out the lights to see how they worked.

I got my chance when I stopped a car for speeding on Route 40 in front of the bowling alley. I hit the lights and it was brighter than daytime out there. They were so bright I couldn't see a thing, so I guess that I must've blinded the driver of the speeding car, as well as any passengers he had with him.

I walked up, got his driver's license and registration and walked back to the front of my car. That's when I found out that these lights weren't just bright, they were hot as hell and really putting out a lotta heat. I was getting ready to write the guy a ticket for speeding, when I noticed that the heat from the lights had caused the paint on the trunk of his car to bubble.

I hurried back up to him, and stuffed his driver's license and registration in his hand. "This is your lucky day," I said. "I just got an emergency call. Have a nice day." A second later I was haulin' ass east on Route 40, hoping the guy wouldn't call the barrack and demand a free paint job, compliments of the State of Maryland.

I never heard anything, so I guess the guy thought escaping the speeding ticket balanced out the paint bubbles.

Sexual Enhancement Supplement

It was very late, probably almost midnight, when I decided to sit down at my computer and order my vitamins. I placed the order and thought that was the end of it, when a bold message suddenly appeared on my screen. "Congratulations! You've been selected to receive a new sexual enhancement supplement."

I sent back that I didn't want it, but they replied that, because of the amount of vitamins I had ordered, it was a free gift. I said I didn't want it, but they insisted that they had no choice but to send the supplement. After, a 15 minute argument, by computer no less, I told them if it would make them feel better to go ahead and send it. Five minutes later, I get another message, telling me that it would be shipped separately from my vitamin order.

A week later my vitamin order arrived and, as usual, my UPS guy dropped the package on the woodpile outside my door. A few days later I came home just around dusk and noticed a package on top of the woodpile. I got out of my car and almost immediately I realized the package had been torn open. When I reached the wood-pile, I saw a raccoon scurry around the corner and that's when I saw that the container of sexual enhancement supplement had been ripped apart. The raccoon had eaten every last tablet, or capsule or whatever they were! So much for my free sexual enhancement supplement.

A few weeks later, I went to the Eastern Shore with Jim and Jody to visit Bob Moore. While sitting in the Subway at the outlet mall, I decided to tell Bob and Jim about the supplement and the raccoon. Of course, we took a booth all the way in the back so we wouldn't disturb any of the customers that happened to come in.

Well, anyway, being the way I am, I decided to spice up the story a little just for entertainment purposes. I told them about the vitamin order and delivery of the sexual enhancement supplement and, from there, adlibbed the rest.

I saw this raccoon running off with what appeared to be a projectile or guided missile of some sort, protruding past the front of his body. A few seconds later I was insanely jealous, because I realized that the "missile" he was lugging was actually a seven-foot erection. The way I knew this was the raccoon tripped over a rock in the front yard and pole vaulted into the barn. For the next two hours

I heard cattle mooing happily and horses neighing, while waiting in line for their turn. The following morning I went outside and he was leaning against a fence post, still showing off this seven-foot hard-on and I was even more jealous. I swear this son-of-a-bitch ran around for weeks servicing every female within miles of my house.

I thought about contacting the Vitamin Company and telling them that a wayward raccoon had eaten my free sexual enhancement supplement, but I changed my mind. I don't think they would've believed me anyway. I mean, not unless I had pictures or videotaped evidence of this creature pole-vaulting around the farm and fields, fornicating with everything from a cow to a field mouse.

Bob Moore had to get into the act and talk about the Viagra and Cialis ads on TV.

"If you have an erection that lasts more then 4 hours contact your doctor. Hell, if I have an erection that lasted for more then 4 hours, I'd stand on a street corner with it hangin' out and a sign saying 'come and get it ladies'."

It never really struck Bob or me that Jimmy seemed to think this whole story was unusually funny. It wasn't until we got up to leave that we found out that two women had listened to our rather animated story.

On our way out of Subway, Jimmy very quietly told us that they sat down in a both on the opposite side of the aisle from us. When they caught the gist of the story, they got up and moved into the booth directly behind us to eavesdrop on our entire conversation. You'd think he would have warned us about this, but he was having too much fun, at our expense, knowing we were being spied on. It was at about this same time that he told us the women were now following us.

I peeked over my shoulder and there they were, grinning and walking about 10 feet behind us. Jimmy wasn't gonna let this go. He said they probably thought that Bob and I were bragging about ourselves, and were going to follow us home, feed us a box of

Viagra and have their way with us.

Hey, I wouldn't mind having a little fun, but I sure as hell can't produce a seven-foot erection and pole vault all the way to the barn. I'd be satisfied if I tripped over the scatter rug and pole vaulted over a beer mug.

Coffee Flavored Car Wash

Back in the "old days" there weren't many places in Howard County to pick up a coffee or sandwich after hours, which meant we had to cross the county line to find an open business. When working Route 1, one of those places was Lucky Days, just over the line in Baltimore County.

Lucky Days didn't exactly serve the best tasting coffee in the world, but if you drank a cup, you could stay awake for a week or so. A lot of us joked that it took about 15 minutes to pour a cup of their coffee, because it was so thick that it just sort of oozed out of the pot and landed with a sick sounding "plop" in the bottom of your cup

It was one of those nights, and I had my Lucky Days coffee in my lap, sitting on Buttermilk Hill in Elkridge, working radar. After a gulp or two of my coffee, my eyes snapped open and I was ready for anything. Of course, I wasn't expecting anything to happen so quickly, but my radar sounded like it had taken a sip of my coffee. Zoom! Ninety-five miles an hour, up Buttermilk Hill, and by me like a shot.

I threw my coffee out the window to give pursuit. Son-of-a-bitch! Dumb shit that I am, I forgot to roll the window down before tossing the coffee. I've got coffee all over the window, the steering wheel and my uniform. I don't know where the hell the cup went, but I'm surprised that it's not hanging on my left ear. Now, I'm pissed and can't get after Rocket Man quick enough, and I was determined that he wasn't gonna get away.

I finally caught up with the guy somewhere well beyond Meadowridge Cemetery and pulled him over. I smelled like a coffee urn, but knew the coffee blended well with the dark brown State Police uniform coat. That's probably why the state chose brown for our uniforms—to hide all the coffee we spilled. Anyway, I got out of my car and approached the driver. He rolled his window down and, after I introduced myself, I started to explain why I'd stopped him. The next thing I knew, it sounded like I was the host of Let's Make a Deal. I told him it was his lucky night and he had a choice. Behind

Door #1, you can choose to accept a summons with a fine in the amount of $500.00. But, behind Door #2, you can opt to follow me to the State Police Barrack, clean my car and we'll forget about the $500.00 summons. In no time at all he accepted the prize behind door #2.

I didn't exactly explain things that way, but he followed me to the barrack and cleaned my car. I only wanted him to wash the window and clean off the steering wheel, but he really got into the job. Before it was over, he had cleaned the entire interior of my cruiser and then went to work washing the exterior. I swear if I hadn't stopped him, I think he would've waxed it too.

He went home happy and I went back to work with a clean car, but I didn't go back to Lucky Days for another coffee. There was no reason to tempt fate twice in the same night. Naturally, that idea went right to hell on my very next stop. I was in such a hurry to get out of the car, I forget to unhook my seatbelt and damn near cut myself in half. That's when I knew it was gonna be a long, long night.

A Woman's Wrath

Kenneth McGlynn

I was working the midnight shift and around 5:30 AM I was dispatched to Main Street for a medical emergency. Someone had called and reported hearing eerie moans and, every now and then, a loud scream coming from the area of the old coal yards. That area is near the river and lined with old buildings, most of which had been abandoned, but were often used for parties and "other activities."

I arrived with the EMTs from Company 2 and we began searching the area, which at the time was very dark. After a few minutes we could hear the moaning and followed it to one of the coal bins. I shined my light around and spotted a man lying on a heap of clothing, clutching his groin. As we got closer, I recognized him as one of our local Main Street gentlemen and thought he was probably suffering from a bad hangover.

One of the EMTs—I think it was Billy Merson, walked over and asked him what was wrong. He didn't say anything. He just held his groin and went on moaning. Billy helped him pull his pants down so he could try to determine the cause and extent of his injury.

I was standing behind the EMTs, holding my flashlight and

suddenly there it was. The cause of his pain made me flinch. The biggest safety pin I had ever seen in my life was sticking through his penis and it was clamped shut. He was bleeding and it looked like the wound was infected. That's when I almost tossed the early breakfast I had eaten, but somehow managed to keep it down.

The "How did this happen" phase of my investigation began, after he was taken to the hospital. He explained that in a lust-crazed moment of insanity he had solicited one of our more famous Main Street "Beauty Queens" for an evening of "romance." She agreed to thrill him with her oral skills, but only as long as he kept his promise of providing her with a bottle of whiskey.

She kept her end of the bargain, but the instant he received his gratification, he ran off with the whiskey. She hunted him down, finding him passed out in the coal bin and took revenge by jabbing the safety pin through his penis and clamping it shut. She proudly bragged over what she had done, and our "man about Main Street" became the safety pin topic of conversation for weeks.

Oh, he decided not to press charges. Although I wish he had. I would have given anything to sit in the courtroom and listen to that testimony.

Driving While…

Evening shift was winding down to a close and I was on Route 108 near Route 29, hoping and praying for a quiet ending. It was the last night, and "Choir Practice" was scheduled, and I was ready for a cold beer. I thought I had everything timed perfectly and hit Route 29, northbound, thinking I was home free.

Within seconds I saw the car. It was only a hundred yards or so in front of me, weaving from lane to lane. *Oh, shit, a DWI,* I thought. I slowed down a little, pulled into the slow lane and so did the car in front of me. Other traffic was beginning to close in around us, and I knew I had to stop the car immediately.

I turned on the overhead lights and instantly there was frantic movement from the car in front of me. Arms and legs were flailing, and then it looked as if someone either jumped or was thrown into the back seat. *Holy shit, what've I got?* I thought as the car pulled to the shoulder. I called for back up units and got out of my car.

I walked very slowly up to the passenger's side of the car, where I could see a young woman in the backseat. When I looked closer, I saw that she was naked from the waist down. I turned my attention to the driver who was leaning over and reaching under the front seat. Naturally, my first thought was that he was reaching for a gun. I pulled my revolver and yelled, "Everybody freeze."

At that instant, the first back up units drove up, and I opened the back door of the car and pulled the young woman out. Other officers yanked the driver's door open and yelled to the driver to get out. Well, he has revolvers and shotguns aimed at him, and he's fumbling around trying to get out. Finally, he stumbled out of the car and stood up.

Well, there he is with spotlights, headlights and flashlights illuminating him, his pants and underwear down around his ankles, and a condom hanging from his penis.

Okay, I thought. *What the hell's going on here?*

It took a few minutes to sort out the details, but it turned into a very interesting tale. Certainly one that would be discussed over those cold beers at "Choir Practice."

The young lady's curfew was fast approaching and they were desperate to make love. But, finding the right location and taking time to enjoy themselves would have caused them to arrive at her house beyond the appointed deadline. So, the next best thing in their young, horny minds, was to "do the deed" while driving home. He pulled over, slid the seat all the way back, and dropped his pants and shorts. She peeled off her skirt and panties, straddled him and he drove off, figuring to satisfy their lustful craving and "beat the clock."

Since there was no alcohol involved, I put forth a courageous effort to give them a stern lecture before sending them on their way. Under the circumstances, it was difficult to deliver a strict reprimand regarding their "driving" habits and do so without laughing.

Curiosity Caused a Problem

It seemed as if it was my destiny to get all of the strange medical assist calls in my assigned area. This call was no different.

I went to meet EMTs at an apartment in Town and Country where a man was complaining of severe abdominal pain.

In the apartment, between groans, the man, who was a pretty big guy, confessed that in an idle moment, he was overwhelmed with curiosity. To satisfy his curiosity he took out his wife's vibrator and began to "experiment" with it. Apparently, he got a far more carried away than he had intended and when he inserted it into his rectum, it shot right in like a suppository.

Now, in complete panic, he wanted me, or the EMTs to reach up in there and pull it out so his wife wouldn't learn of his curious game. We looked at each other with a "Yeah, pal, like we're gonna do that" look, and told him he was going to the hospital. There, he could get professional help in removing his wife's vibrator.

He was taken to Howard County General Hospital and later that evening, I had to go there to complete an accident investigation. I thought while I was there, I'd check on him as well. By now, he and his tale of the afternoon's curious experimentation were the topic of conversation among doctors and nurses. Naturally, all of his X-rays showing the vibrator and its final resting-place made their "Highlight Reel."

Burglar in the House

Sheldon Greenberg

It had been a relatively quiet Sunday morning, until the radio's emergency alert tone sounded and shattered the calm. The dispatcher's voice followed, announcing a Breaking and Entering in progress at a home near Wilde Lake. The dispatcher advised that, according to the reporting person, the suspect was in the house at that time. I arrived on the scene within minutes, followed by other responding officers.

Corporal Ed Geisler was the area supervisor and, after a brief conversation, a perimeter was set up around the house. I asked for a description of the suspect, but was told none had been provided. I entered the residence with Corporal Geisler and Officer Roberts, after having been informed by the dispatcher that the occupant of the home, a 14-year old boy had gone next door to a neighbor's house.

We began a cautious search of the interior of the home, looking for the burglar.

We conducted a room-by-room search, carefully checking inside closets, under beds and looking for any place the suspect might hide. Our initial search turned up nothing and the only place we hadn't looked was the attic. Although there was no evidence showing that the overhead door had been opened, the attic would still have to be searched.

Corporal Geisler devised a plan of action and decided that Officer Roberts would enter the attic first, and we would act as back up. Just as we were preparing to enter the attic, the young boy, who called the police, came back home.

I first asked if he was okay and he said, "Yes." Then I asked if the suspect had fled the home before we arrived. He gave me a rather funny look, but said, "No."

I told him we had searched the house and found nothing, but that we would go ahead and check the attic to be certain the burglar wasn't up there.

"Burglar? What burglar?"

"We were dispatched here for a report of a Breaking and Entering, and we were told the burglar was in the house."

The boy shook his head. "I didn't call and report a Breaking and Entering."

"You didn't call and tell the dispatcher that there was a burglar in your house."

"No, sir. I called and said there was a bird in the house. I just wanted to know how I could get it out, that's all."

Somehow, when the boy called, "bird" became "burglar" to the call taker, and the boy was told to flee the residence and go next door for his own safety. I could only imagine what he must have been thinking when a half dozen police officers arrived, set up a perimeter, and searched his home for a bird. And, a bird we didn't find.

I'm Gonna Win 10 Million Dollars

Ed Puls, with a little help from his friends

Life was never boring in the Crime Lab, but some days it seemed like we were being visited by aliens or that some of the chemicals had seeped into a few brain stems.

I'm uncertain if it was an alien visitation, or chemical distress that caused John, our photo tech, to announce that he was going to win 10 million dollars. But, he was sure he was going from rags to riches, because he had just received a Publisher's Clearinghouse notification that he *could* be the next big winner.

I tried to tell John that he wasn't going to win 10 million dollars, just because he got a letter in the mail saying he could be the next winner of the grand prize. "John, thousands, maybe millions of people get the same letter every year. It's doesn't mean they're going to win the grand prize."

"It's signed by Ed McMahon," he said.

"John, I don't care if it's signed by the Pope, you aren't gonna win the big one."

"No, I'm gonna win 10 million dollars." He dropped the

letter on my desk and pointed. "Right there, it says I'll be notified on May 27th that I've won."

Well, that's not the way I read the letter, but nothing I, or anyone else said would change his mind. He went to everybody in the police station, no matter where he or she was, carrying the letter and telling him or her he was going to win this multi-million dollar jackpot. He cornered people in the lobby, the hallways, parking lot, by the vending machines and even the men's room.

The day after he strolled in with the letter and announced that he would be the next big winner, I overheard him talking on the telephone. I couldn't believe my ears. He was on the phone to the IRS asking them how much he would have to pay in taxes on his winnings!

After hanging up with the IRS, he submitted a leave request to Sergeant Lilley, asking to have off on May 27th. However, he made up some lame excuse as to why he wanted off, but everyone knew that he was going to sit home and wait for the call from Ed McMahon, telling him he'd won. His leave was approved.

By May 27th everybody in the building was relieved that he was off. At least, we wouldn't have to listen to his daily babbling about the 10 million dollars he was going to win. Believe me, his constant, almost nonstop chatter about winning the jackpot was grating on everyone's nerves.

Somewhere around 10:00 AM, Sergeant Lilley said he sure hated to think of John sitting by the phone and not getting a call from Ed McMahon. That sounded like a hint to me. So, I went to the Crime Prevention Office and asked Cathy to come to the Crime Lab for an "important meeting." In no time at all, she agreed to take part in the "Ed McMahon Sweepstakes" and call John.

We were in a position to hear only one side of the telephone conversation, but it was truly most interesting. When John answered the telephone, which he did almost instantly, she introduced herself as Ed McMahon's personal secretary. "Sir, for… Sir, we'll get to the prize you've won in a minute. Sir, for our records, I'd like to get some information…" She paused, trying not to laugh. "Sir, I need to get this information before I can tell you what prize you've won."

Finally, she settled John down enough to give her what she had been asking for. She did a fantastic job, playing the role of Ed McMahon's personal secretary. She asked John about his career, his family and hobbies. Then came the big moment.

"Our judges work long hours deciding on prizes and how they should be awarded. You, sir, have won... No, sir, you did not win the 10 million dollars. You have won an all expenses paid trip for two, to beautiful, scenic downtown Sykesville, Maryland.* A pause. "No sir, you cannot exchange it for something else." Pause. "Sir, I can't help it if you live near Sykesville and drive through, or by it every day. This is the prize you've won."

When Cathy ended the call, John immediately called Captain Jack Burke, the Commander of the Criminal Investigations Bureau to tell him about the prize he'd won.

Of course, Captain Jack knew damn well that John had been set up by the gang in the Crime Lab, and told him what had really happened.

A few minutes after he called Captain Jack, John called the Crime Lab. "I knew it was you guys all along. I knew right away that it was Denny's wife, Robin, who called me. I recognized her voice the second I answered the phone. I just played along with the joke."

Yes, John, and I'm gonna win the next big 10 million dollar prize.

*Sykesville, Maryland is a small, quiet town, where Main Street is just a little longer than a city block.

More Life and Times in the Maryland State Police

With Trooper First Class Don Newcomer, assisted by Peter F. Edge and some that hope to remain anonymous.

Hot Wheels to Hoofin' It

I was assigned to the Westminster Barrack as a Criminal Investigator under the Resident Trooper Program. As such, I was given a brand new Dodge St. Regis, which immediately pissed everybody off, because they didn't want me to have it. Of course, the lieutenant was really pissed, because he thought he should have the car, but since the county put up the money, the car went to the Resident Trooper.

One day I stopped by to see if the repair work had been completed on my lawn mower. Well, it was done and, rather than drive home, get the truck and come back, I thought I'd haul it in the St. Regis. I opened the trunk and tried to put in there, but it wouldn't fit. So, I rolled the back windows down, set it on the back seat and took off down the road with the handle hangin' out the window.

While heading down the road, I was intercepted by my

corporal, who wanted to know how in the hell I got it in the back seat, and why it was in the St. Regis. I said, "I tried, but it wouldn't fit in the trunk."

The next thing you know, I'm standing there in front of the lieutenant and he says I'm to be punished. He orders a 30-day punishment period, meaning I'm not to drive the St. Regis and I had to furnish my own transportation to the barrack. To really put the screws to me, he said if he heard me calling any other troopers to provide transportation to and from work, he'd take the car away for another 30 days.

I said, "Fine, that's what we'll do."

The second day of my car suspension, the lieutenant comes into the barrack and I came in right behind him. Naturally, there was no exchange of sweet nothings in our passing. But when lunchtime rolled around, he walked outside and found a mule tied securely to the bumper of his police car, and the mule had shit everywhere.

I had followed him outside and he turns to me and says, "What's the meaning of this?"

"Well, Lieutenant, you told me I had to provide my own transportation and, this morning, my car wouldn't start. So, I rode ole Jack here to work."

"Well, you get Jack's ass offa my bumper."

"Lieutenant, first I wanna warn you that those meadow muffins really screw up a spit-shine. I know how proud you are of your shoe shine, so be careful not to step in any of those muffins."

Well, after 15 days he relented and gave my St. Regis back. He said I was too much of a headache and pain in the ass."

I didn't ride Jack all the way from my house to work. I put him on a truck and drove him to the parking lot of a business next door to the barrack. Then I saddled him up, and rode on to the barrack dressed in full State Police Uniform.

North East Lady of the Evening

Pete and I went to North East, Maryland with a gang of our

guys because of a prostitution ring operating there. This bunch of hookers had been arrested in Delaware and Pennsylvania and the Delaware State Police said if we could bust them in Maryland, federal charges could be filed.

We went up there as workers for the Lawrence Construction Company, named for our Captain, Will Lawrence. We got in this flea-bitten motel, and that's probably a kind description of the place. Hell, the fleas were so big I don't think two of 'em could've gotten in the bathtub together. And, I don't mean to be too disrespectful to the fleas, but that just gives you an idea of what this place was like. Anyway, we parked our very plain cars, got a room and made our calls.

Pretty soon these three or four girls show up, and when they got there, I mean they were ragged lookin' bastards. Ole Petey, over there, is lookin' at this one and she says I gotta get something to drink. So Petey, ever the gentleman, takes her to the nearest package goods store.

They go in to shop and she bends over and her breasts fall outta her shirt. All these hillbillies are starin' and Petey thinks he's gonna get killed by hillbilly slobber before he gets outta there. Well, that's because she just walks around the store with 'em hangin' out and makes no effort to stuff 'em back in her shirt.

When they get back, the girl wants me to jump in and do the thing with her, but I said, "Hold on a second. Petey's my boss and he's my best friend. Can Petey come over too?"

She says, "Well, I've never done this before, but for another seventy-five, I'll do ya both."

We get in the room and I turn to Petey. "Look, you've gotta realize that I'm the one that brought ya into this, but I'm gonna be first."

"Now you hold on just a darn minute. I'm your boss."

"Come on, boss. I try to remember you, now you remember me."

"No," Petey says. "No, it's gonna be me first."

46

Well, we're standin' there and I don't know what the hell she was wearin', but she's got one zipper on this outfit. I mean, one pull and she's totally naked—panties, bra, everything. Then, she trots off to the bathroom.

While she's in there, Pete says, "Look, Donny, you gotta get undressed real slow. We've gotta get her to tell us exactly what she's gonna do."

"Okay."

She comes outta the bathroom and flops on to the bed. And, this bitch stunk. I mean that gal smelled bad.

All along, Pete and I had been using the best hillbilly accents we could muster and I looked at him. "Now, Petey, let me get this straight. Are you gonna be first, or am I gonna be first."

"No, no, I already told ya. I'm gonna be first. You're gonna be second. So, you get in the bathroom and close the door."

"Oh, come on, Petey, can't I watch?"

"No you can't watch. This is between her and me."

So, she's getting' pissed and yells, "Listen, one of you son-of-a-bitches get over here and do somethin'. I'm gettin' mighty tired of talkin' about it."

I said, "Alright, Petey, I'll go in the bathroom."

I went in the bathroom, but I didn't close the door all the way. There was a crack in the door and I put my eye up to the opening and I couldn't resist. "Petey. Oh, Petey, I'm a watchin' you."

"You son-of-a-bitch," he yelled. "Close that door and quit lookin'."

"Petey, I just got to see this. I wanna see a fat boy screw this girl. That's exactly what I wanna see."

Finally, he just forgets about me and turns back to her and says, "Now what I can I do to ya?" Of course, to make the case, we had to get her to tell us what she was gonna do. He says to her, "Can I get a blowjob?"

"No, I only do that to my boyfriend."

"Well, can I have rectal sex?"

"No, I only do that with my boyfriend."

He shrugs and says, "Okay, just what will you do?"

She says, "For Christ's sake, I'll fuck ya, just get on it."

Pete gives her a grin. "Honey, I hate to do this to ya." And, with that, he reaches in his pocket and pulls out his badge.

"You dumb son-of-a-bitch, where'd you get that badge?" She yells. "You ain't no damn cop."

With that, I stepped out of the bathroom and he says, "You see the hands on that monkey. He's gonna put his hands around your throat and choke the shit outta you if you make any noise."

She says, "I guess he's got a badge too." Well, I pulled mine out to show her and she yells, "Just where did you dumb son-of-a-bitches get these State Police Badges? I know you're not cops."

We finally convinced her to get dressed and then we arrested her. That's when she said, "I've never seen so damn much belly and so little pecker in my life." And, when we took her to court, she told the judge the same thing.

Pete jumps in and says, "What Donny's not telling you is, that when we first get to North East, there's a guy—these kids come runnin' in, and say there's a man in the phone booth with a gun."

They say he's wearing a leather coat and he has a gun. Well, that's gotta be the pimp for the girls we called, and he has the gun because he's their protector.

Donny goes out to the phone booth, grabs this guy and spins him around. He grabs his coat to pull it up to check for the gun and promptly rips it all the way up to the guy's neck.

Hey, I approached the guy and said the word is, you're here with these girls. If that's the case I need to see some ID. He said, "Go fuck yourself." Well, that was the wrong thing to say. This was a big guy too and I wasn't takin' any chances. I spun him around and the next thing you know his jacket rips all the way up above the shoulders. I whacked him too and put his ass on the ground. I mean this was a monstrous guy. He was about 6'5" and weighed about 300 pounds. So, he got whacked. He got slammed and he got cuffed. Then we decided it was getting late, so we just took the cuffs off and sent him home, and he was fine with that.

That was a different time back then. We worked together, looked out for each other and had fun doing the job.

Forecast: Outhouse Showers

We had a trooper named "Bull Ass" Morgan. Actually that was his nickname. His real name was Gary Morgan, and he was what we called a racetrack derelict. Gary got transferred to work undercover, and assigned to the racetrack, which was the worst thing they could do.

It took him two and a half hours just to drive to work every day and, the first thing he'd do every morning, when he arrived was head to the men's room. He'd get in there and plant his ass on a commode and, like clockwork, every morning I'd follow him into the men's room. There were three stalls in there and, whatever one he'd get in, I'd get in the one beside him with a cup of water.

I had a way I'd screw with everybody. I'd tell them to "say it" meaning I wanted to hear them say "I wuv you, Uncle Donny." Anyway, I'd pop over the top of the stall and hold the cup of water over Gary's head and "whisper" those magic words, "say it."

Well, this one morning, I held the cup over his head and said, "Gary, say it."

He sits there and says, "No. I ain't sayin' that shit any more."

"Now, Gary, say it and say it with feeling."

"Damn it, Newcomer, I ain't sayin' that dumb shit any more."

"Look, Gary, say 'I wuv you, Uncle Donny."

"Fuck you, I'm not sayin' I wuv you."

So, I spilled a little water on him.

"All right, you son-of-a-bitch—I wuv you, Uncle Donny."

This went on for months. And, I mean, every time he went in there, I'd be right behind him with a cup of water. Finally, it got to the point where he said, "Screw you. Go ahead and gimme a shower. I'm not sayin' that dumb shit any more."

Some time after this, I walked into the barrack to get ready for court. I'm dressed casual, wearing khaki pants and loafers and, all of a sudden, I see opportunity presenting itself right there in front of me. So, I went into one of the rooms where Gary is, and I say, "Damn, I've gotta go to court and I got a case of the runnin' shits. I'm gonna have to hit the men's room again before I get outta here." I groan a little and grab my stomach to make it look more realistic, and run outta the room.

A minute later, Gary hurries down the hallway carrying a big ass coffeepot full of water. He pushes the men's room door open and bends down to get a look under the stall doors. The next thing you know he charges in, jumps up on the commode beside the occupied stall, yells "take this you son-of-a-bitch" and dumps the whole damn pot of water.

He runs back out into the hallway and sees me standing there and he realizes he's screwed up. That's when I told him I saw the Captain, who none of us really liked that much, walkin' down the hallway toward the men's room. He was wearing khaki pants and loafers that looked almost exactly like mine. As usual, he had a big cigar stuffed in his jaw and a newspaper tucked up under his arm. I said, "So, Gary, it looks like the captain was in there takin' a shit."

"Here, take this," he said, trying to give me the coffeepot.

"You're outta your mind if think I'm puttin' my fingerprints all over that damn coffeepot."

At that very moment, Gary ran out of the building and I knew I just couldn't pass this up. I walked into the men's room just as the captain was coming out of the stall. His hair was hanging down in his face and water's just dripping off of him like a waterfall. His cigar is soaked and drooping below his chin, and he's holdin' this soggy newspaper in his hand.

I looked at him and said, "Damn, Captain, you always sweat

that much when you're havin' a bowel movement?"

He didn't say a word and I took that as my cue to leave for court. But, not a thing was ever said about what happened. The captain never tried to track down all of us who were involved, or ask for any disciplinary action.

Undercover Hallucination

We had a guy—for the purpose of the story, I'll just call him Dick—screaming to be assigned to the undercover unit. Well, Dick screamed everything from prejudice to personal grudges as reasons for his request being denied. But the truth is, he was just dumb as shit. He was a stupid son-of-bitch who couldn't even do the job while working in uniform. Eventually, I guess they got tired of listening to his complaints and assigned him to undercover work.

He's only in the unit a week or so and comes downstairs, looks right at me and says, "Hey, guys, there's a contract on my life."

I looked at him and said, "You silly bastard, you haven't done anything to warrant a contract on your life."

"Well, I bought those stolen batteries at that junk yard up in Hagerstown, and that guy wants to have me killed."

"Dick, get real. It's all bullshit. Nobody really gives a rat's ass about you buying batteries, especially that guy."

That issue went away, but all of sudden, Dick starts to get this feeling that he's really worthy of being an undercover trooper, and he hasn't done jack-shit. Now, our desks are pushed up against each other, and he's sittin' there one day, kinda slinked down in his chair. He looks over at me and says, "You know, Newcomer, if this was Vietnam, you know what I'd do?"

"I have no idea, Dick."

"In Vietnam, I'd just take my .45 and I'd just shoot you right in your fuckin' head."

I looked over at him. "Is that right?"

"Yeah, you think you're so damn tough."

"No, Dick, you're wrong. I don't think I'm tough at all," I said, standing up and stepping into my chair. I put one foot on my desk and the other foot on his desk. Then I stepped over and put my foot right down on his nuts. I leaned down, grabbed him by the throat and jerked him up outta the chair. "Now, Dick, I'm gonna show you what life's all about." It's rainin' cats and dogs and Dick is now backed right up to the basement door. I opened the door and threw his ass right out in the pouring rain.

He starts bangin' on the door and screamin', "Come on, Newt, I was only kiddin'. I was only kiddin'."

I said, "I was only kiddin' too, Dick."

"Let me in."

I laughed and said, "Tell me what I wanna hear."

"What the hell do you wanna hear?"

"I wanna hear 'I wuv you, Uncle Donny'."

By now his ass is soaked and he says, "I wuv you, Uncle Donny."

"Now, now, Dick. Say it with sincerity. You don't sound like you really mean it."

So he gives his best effort at being sincere and says, "I wuv you, Uncle Donny."

"The only way you're gonna get in, is go up the back steps and come in."

Dick goes up the back steps of the Waterloo Barrack and right down the hall to the captain's office—Captain Will Lawrence. Will's really the greatest guy in the world to work for and he comes downstairs with Dick—a very wet Dick, right behind him.

Captain Lawrence looks at me and says, "Newt, did you throw Dick out the back door into the wet weather?"

I stood up and said, "Captain, this is exactly what I did." I grabbed Dick by the throat and threw his ass right out the back door, into the pouring again.

Captain Lawrence nods and says, "You know, Newt, you do that really good." He turned around and left and that was the end of it.

Eventually the powers that be realized that, as an undercover trooper and probably as a trooper in general, Dick wasn't smart enough to pull his pecker outta his pants before he took a piss. So, his days of basking in self-made glory came to an end. If he asked, Pete and I would've gladly helped him empty his desk.

The Viagra Switch

I was sitting at home one day when I got a call from my son who works for Homeland Security. One of our former sergeants with the Maryland State Police approached him and asked him to ask me if I had any Viagra. If so, he wanted me to give it to my son to bring to him at work, because he had a "hot one" lined up for the next night.

I looked at my son and said, "By God, he's got a pharmacy program and probably the same one I've got. If he's in such dire need for Viagra for this hot date, he can get it himself."

But, I decided that it was time to have some fun. I went into the bathroom and took out a bottle of pills, which were Tylenol PM and, of course, they are blue in color.

I sent them over to him, with a message that they were only 50 milligrams and that he should take all four.

He popped the four pills when he's leaving work and goes over to dazzle her with his powerful erection and lovemaking skills. Well, he gets all fired up and climbs on to give her the ride of her life and he falls asleep.

He called me the next day and said, "You common son-of-a-bitch. What the fuck did you do to me?"

"What are you talkin' about? I sent you the Viagra you asked for."

"Well, I climbed on and fell sound asleep. Christ, I woke up all groggy and had to stumble outta her place to get home."

"Serves you right, you prick. They were Tylenol PM. If you

want Viagra, go buy it yourself."

Hand Off

Pete Edge fall guy for Donny

I was with Donny, and I believe we were down in Arkansas. Donny was workin' the computer, because me and computers don't really get along. I mean I'm lucky I can even turn one on. Anyway, we were up to our ass in alligators busy and Donny's sittin' there at the computer putting all the information in, while I roll everybody's fingerprints. This was a FEMA job we were on, and it required taking personal information and rolling a set of prints to make sure everybody was who they were supposed to be.

Well, I needed to take a break and run to the John before I cut loose and drown everybody in the place. I raised my hand and said, "Donny, may I?" and he was nice enough to let me go. Forty-seven gallons later, I'm back and ready to roll more prints.

I'm not really paying attention to what's going on, because after a while the routine is just that—a routine. I'm like a robot doing the same thing over and over. I reached back for the next guy's hand and he gives it to me and I start to roll his prints.

Pretty soon Donny's not just laughing his ass off, he's howling. Everybody in the place is going crazy laughing and I haven't got a damn clue about what's so funny. So, I started to turn around to see what they're all laughing at, and I see that I'm just holding a hand. I mean that's all I had, a hand and several inches of wrist.

While I was in the John, Donny and the next guy in line for fingerprints, set me up. He'd had part of his lower arm and hand amputated and when I said, "Next" he just gave me his hand.

"Yeah, and Pete almost finished rolling the whole set of prints before he knew what was going on."

"Well, besides that, they were best set of prints I'd ever rolled."

"When we go on these trips, I always pick Pete to go on my team because of the entertainment factor. We were on one of these outings and something happened and I went to Pete's room around 10:00 PM. I knocked on the door and I hear this 'yeah' from inside."

So I said, "Come on, Pete, open the door."

There's some shuffling around and he opens the door and I damn near fell over at the sight. "He's got this pair of nylons, held up with garters and…"

"Damn it, Donny, they were diabetes socks."

"The garters are up to his knees and he's wearing these Hawaiian underpants and this machine… What'd you call it?"

"It's a C-Pap Machine (for treating sleep disorders)."

"This C-Pap Machine is on his head and his hair's sticking out." Now, I'm laughing at the sight and finally I'm able to say, "Tell me, Pete, how in the hell do you ever get laid?"

Pete says, "They're all pity humps. Hey, guys, even if they weren't gorgeous, at least they were all alive."

"Well, Pete, that's good to know."

Mayonnaise Riot

We went into Baltimore City during the riots and one of our guys, Dominic, who just passed away, saw a gang that had just cleaned out a supermarket. I mean they had stolen every last item in the store. This great big fat bitch is runnin' down the street and she's got a gallon of mayonnaise underneath her dress. I guess she's runnin' with it between her legs, but I don't know for sure. And, I don't know how in the hell she can run, but she's just humpin' down the street.

Well, Dominic goes after her because he's not gonna allow everybody to get away. He's gaining on her and, all of a sudden, the mayonnaise jar slips out from under her dress, hits the street and breaks. Dominic runs right into this pile of mayonnaise and glass, but somehow he manages to get grab a hold of this woman. He's trying to dig his heels in and stop, but it's like he's wearin' ice skates. He keeps trying to dig his heels in and it seems like he's got flames flyin' outta the bottom of his shoes, while she's draggin his ass up the street.

The rest of us are laughin' so hard at Dominic, we can't even run to help him make the arrest.

Then I turned around and saw a guy come running out of a pharmacy. He ran out through what used to be the plate glass window in the front of the store. He took off up the street and I went after him. He tried to get away from me by diving down a flight of stairs. There were only three steps down, a platform and three steps up. Well, this guy knocked himself out when he hit the steps. I patted him down and he had a load of drugs on him that he'd stolen from the pharmacy. So, I picked him up and lugged his ass down to the lockup.

By now, he's awake and figures he's gotta put on a show for three other maggots who're sittin' in the cell. The door hasn't been closed yet, and he steps up and says, "If you didn't have that badge and gun on, I'd kick your fuckin' ass."

Well, I took off my badge and gun, handed them over to a Baltimore City Officer and said, "You're never gonna get another opportunity like this." I walked into the cell and landed a punch square on his nose. He went down on his ass and stayed there, so I turned to the other three. "Anybody else wanna a little of this?"

"No, sir, Boss," one of 'em said. "We ain't that stupid."

At this point Pete joined in. "I just loved workin' with the Baltimore City Police. They were the greatest guys. It was great to see how they handled some of the real hard asses. They had a few in the back of the wagon that just wouldn't shut up. They kept on and on about kickin' everybody's ass and how they were gonna fuck us up. The next thing I know, the driver slams the door and locks 'em in there. He takes off like a shot and then hits the brakes. Takes off again and hits the brakes. Takes off and hits the brakes. Now you know those assholes in the back were rollin' around like bowling balls. But, when he opened the door again, they were just as polite as they could be.

Donny laughed. That was about the end of it for me and Pete and a few others. Baltimore City Police took care of everything—

paperwork, fingerprints, photographs, charging documents and the court testimony. Probably one of the easiest assignments I ever worked.

Country Law

You know, "back when" was a different time and everything sure as hell wasn't done by the book. I guess you might say that sometimes the book was just tossed by the side of the road, and we took care of things. But, we took care of things in a way that the troublemakers understood and most times, when matters were settled, we didn't have a problem with 'em again. And, most of the ones I dealt with, black or white were just as happy to have Uncle Donny hold roadside court and settle things informally. A swift boot in the ass beat the hell outta havin' to hire a lawyer, and standin' in front of a judge, where they could be ordered to pay a fine, which they probably didn't have the money to pay, or end up in jail.

Every now and then though, some assholes would come along who thought that because they were from Baltimore City or Sandy Spring, they could tell me and other troopers, or Howard County officers to "fuck off" and do what they damn well pleased.

The bars in Sykesville, down at the Howard County/Carroll County line, seemed like an attraction that these assholes couldn't resist. They'd show up and stir up a bunch of shit and think they could get away with it.

One night, I was working the midnight shift and a trooper, who had worked the late shift, said, "Newt, we could've used you earlier." Then he told me about a problem the county police had down at the bars in Sykesville, because a few fights had broken out.

I said, "You can't let shit like that happen." Well, before I could say anything else, the county police called a Signal 13 in Sykesville. I grabbed this trooper and said, "Come on, let's go."

We pulled up and I got outta the car, after I grabbed my shotgun from under the headrest. I walked over to a black guy who's sittin' in his car in front of Milt and Joe's. I'll never forget it. He was drivin' a 1957, Grey and White, Ford Station Wagon. So I said, "Buddy, the best thing you can do is crank that thing up and get outta here."

He looked up at me and said, "What did you say, mutha fucker?"

I put the shotgun right in his throat. "You son-of-a-bitch, there's two ways outta here."

"I'm leavin' now," he says, and cranks it up and drives off.

I walked inside the bar, jacked a round in the shotgun and it got instantly quiet. It was so quiet you could've heard a mouse fart. I said, "Okay, this place is now closed." I went over and took the license off the wall. There were some Howard County Officers in there too and, pretty soon, everybody cleared outta the bar.

I walked outside and there had to be over 300 people on the parking lot. So I walked over to the group and said, "Most of you guys know me on a first name basis. If you don't want your asses locked up, get in your cars, crank 'em and go."

Well, they said, "Yes, sir, Mr. Newcomer. Yes, sir, Trooper Newcomer. Yes, sir, Mr. Don, we're leavin'." And, they got in their cars and left.

But, there's a group of about 30 that moved to the Sykesville side of the bar and started yellin'. "You come on over here, mutha fucker. We'll cut your dick off."

So, I yelled to 'em. "Hold the thought."

When everybody else had cleared out, I walked back there. I had my shotgun and I said, "Where's that bad son-of-a-bitch that's gonna de-dick me?"

One of says, "Come on down here."

This core was from Montgomery County and Baltimore City, and they just didn't understand Country Law. So, I raised the shotgun and put a round of double ought buck right over their heads. "I missed you on purpose with that first one, but the next one's gonna hit the ground in front of you. It's gonna take your shins, your knees and there's gonna be bones hangin' and you're gonna be a crippled bunch of sons-of-bitches."

They all turned and started runnin'. They ran down the embankment, and crossed the river. Now, they're bustin' their asses tryin' to climb up over the rocks and stones on the other side, toward Southern States.

I yelled, "Where's that bad ass son-of-a-bitch that was gonna de-nut me? I don't see you any more."

I let another round go over their heads, and it hit the rocks above 'em. And it was about that time that Howard County Officer, Griff Jones comes runnin' around the corner.

He says, "Goddamn, Donny, if you can do it. So can I."

I put a box of shotgun shells on the ground between us and said, "Load up, boy.

But, try not to hit any of those bastards. Let's just scare 'em the hell outta here."

We shot a box of shells between us and by now, everything's shut down. You couldn't even hear a peep and there wasn't a soul to be seen anywhere.

The next morning, I was gettin' ready to go home and just about 8:30 or so the lieutenant gives me a call and says come to the barrack. So, I mumbled, "Oh, shit."

I got in the car and drove to the barrack and the first thing he says is, "What happened in Sykesville last night?"

"Ah, hell, some of the assholes were gettin' restless."

"Was there any gunfire down there?"

I said, "No, sir. I was the first on the scene when the trouble call came in and I was the last to leave. I never heard one gun shot."

"Okay. That's all I needed to know." And, he sent out a report to that effect.

I can tell you, the boys from Baltimore City and Montgomery weren't so brave after that. They just had to have an understanding of Country Law.

Serving Time with Uncle Donny

Pete goes to jail with Donny

You know, now and then we'd get sent to jail to do some undercover job. Well, Donny's big enough that he always started trouble. He'd go over and grab some big son-of-a-bitch and point to me and say, "See that guy over there. He wants to play kissy-face with you. He really does."

I'm terrified, because I just know that I'm gonna get bent over a table, or a sink or something and poked in the ass.

On this trip to jail with Donny, there was this big fat guy, one of the guards that kept knockin' me down. I mean, he would do this every damn day and I was gettin' more than a little tired of his daily bullshit, but he just kept it up. And, I certainly can't jump up and say, "Hey, you fat ignorant pile of whale shit, I'm an undercover Maryland State Trooper. Knock it off."

One day I was shackled to this guy, and on my way to court, and fat ass knocks me down again. Anyway, by now I've been in there longer than I was supposed to be. So, I'm beginning to think that the assholes that sent me on this assignment forgot about me, or they're just leavin' me here on purpose. Well, I picked myself up off the floor to go to court, where I'm supposed to be shipped back to North Carolina because I had murdered a friend down there.

But right now, all I can think is, *If I ever get outta here, I'm gonna find this fat fuckin' guard and stomp his ass.*

I finally got out and I waited about two months, while very quietly doing all the research to find out where this guard lived. One morning I'm waiting outside his house, dressed in black from head to toe, and here comes blubber ass, waddling home. I beat the shit outta this asshole. I never said a word like, "Hey, this is from me" or anything like that. I just pummelled the shit outta him.

Then I took off runnin' and damned near killed myself gettin' back to my car, because I parked it about a mile a way. And you know I'm not a runner. My fastest time in the mile is six months. But, I never did hear a word about what happened to the guy.

After all the shit this guard pulled, they probably had a list of suspects a mile long and didn't even think of me.

Eastern Shore Triple Header

Donny back in the slammer

I was sent to the Eastern Shore to get information on a triple homicide. They had a guy locked up and they were sure he knew about this triple homicide. He was in jail on armed drug trafficking charges and I was told that he used to build and race rail cars. His name was Donny and he was just a little fart.

Well, they put me in a special cell with this little shit, and he tells me he's a born again Christian. He tells me that once he gets this mess behind him, that he's really gonna take off on a new life.

"That's good," I said.

He had a wall covered with pictures of his rail cars. Along with all these pictures he's got newspaper clippings and pictures of his wife. Well, one Sunday I'm stretched out on the bunk and his wife walks in. She strolls up to the bars and he reaches through and grabs her ass. Then he starts fondling her tits, looks at me and says, "Isn't she wonderful?"

"Yeah, she looks pretty good. But, you're not exactly actin' the way I expected a Christian to act. But, I guess that's what you do."

Before he can say anything she says, "Hey, Honey, there's something I've gotta tell you."

He says, "What's that?"

"The Mac Tool man came this week and repossessed all your tools."

"Mutha fucker took my tools," he yells.

"Yes, he took all your tools and that's not the worst part."

He looks at her and says, "Well, what's the worst part?"

"The Pepsi man came and took our machine and all of our stock."

"Son-of-a-bitch," he screams.

I'm up there on the bunk, laughin' my ass off and I just had to do it. I said, "Donny, where's all that Christian love you had last week?"

The next thing you know, and before he answers, we're told we have to be moved to another cell. The one they had us housed in was actually for women, and they arrested some women and needed the cell. We were marched off to the Bullpen, where there were two black guys. One was a rather big, burly guy and the other one was this skinny little cocksucker, and I mean that was his persuasion.

When we get in the cell, Donny runs over and jumps on the bottom bunk. I said, "Get your ass off that bunk. You're up above."

I stretched out on the bottom bunk and this skinny little black guy comes over and says, "Hi, fella, how're you?"

"I'm really good," I said. "But, there's two things I really hate. One's blacks and the other's faggots. So, you best back the fuck off. But, the guy up there, he likes both."

Donny's up there and he's got the blanket all the way up under his chin. Well, this guy climbs up and gets in the bunk with him.

Donny starts screamin', "Get the hell away from me you son-of-a-bitch. Can't you feel I'm a Christian?"

After they moved us out of the Bullpen, and back to our "private cell" I got enough information out of him to have him charged as accessory to the three murders. He didn't take part in them, but he did help dispose of the bodies.

Emergency Road Service

Officer David Cogle and friends.

I had planned to meet some friends for a celebration after working my evening shift with the Baltimore County Police. The only drawback was the party was being held on the East Side of Baltimore. I could take the long way, and drive all the way around the Baltimore Beltway, or take the direct route through the heart of the city. After thinking about it, I decided to go through the city and save time.

It was a chilly evening and the pedestrian traffic was almost non-existent and, in fact, there wasn't a lot of vehicle traffic. I was making pretty good time, and I was about half way through the city when my right rear tire blew out. I wasn't happy about having to change a tire in my present location, but I sure as hell just couldn't sit there and hope for a tow truck to appear.

I was beginning to jack up the Jeep, when two of Baltimore's more upstanding citizens walked by. They looked me over, directed a few obscene comments my way, crossed the street and stood on the corner watching me. I kept working the jack, but now I was also trying to keep an eye on them. Pretty soon, they were walking back toward me again, slowing down as they got close. They muttered a few more obscene pleasantries and really looked me over.

I knew what they were thinking. They figured here I was all alone, with a flat tire in the middle of Baltimore City, and an easy mark. And I knew they weren't gonna let the opportunity pass them by. As soon as they reached the curb behind me, they turned and started back. This time they acted as though they were gonna pass on by, but they stopped, with their hands in their pockets as if they were holding guns.

One of them said, "Hey, mutha fucker, you got any money."

A second later they were staring down the barrel of my Sig Sauer P226. "No, but I'm lookin' at two assholes who are gonna change my tire."

At first, I don't think they believed it. Here they were with the odds two to one in their favor, with a lone mark on the streets of Baltimore. Then they were on their knees, changing a flat tire, while their intended victim held a gun to their heads.

They changed the flat in near record time, but I wasn't gonna turn my back on them and try to drive away. I ordered them to stand in front of my car and, after I started the engine, I yelled to them to walk down the street in front of me. So, there we were, just the three of us, enjoying the sights of the city—them walking and me driving. At some point, they decided it was time to get the hell out of there and broke away on a dead run toward an alley.

A moment later, they vanished into the darkness and I was on my way, once again, to meet my friends. I guess I was neglectful in not thanking them for stopping to offer a helping hand in my hour of need but, under the circumstances, it slipped my mind. And, I know could've taken their names and addresses and mailed them a check, but what the hell, maybe next time.

64

Caution: Skunk – Take One

Sergeant Jim Lilley and a cast of unknown parties

I gained a valuable lesson regarding skunks by reading Mark Trail in the Sunday morning comic section of the Washington Post. According to Mr. Trail there are two common varieties of skunks— the ones most of us see, with those two wide white stripes down their backs and another, which is solid black and with only a white tip on the end of their tails. Of the two, the ones with the double white stripes are the more aggressive, and will stand their ground. That's the reason they usually end up dead on the roadways, because when a car suddenly approaches, the skunk stands his or her ground and loses the battle with the automobile. Of course, they will also defend their turf when approached by the human species and, if a human gets too close, will unleash a burst of that "fragrant essence" we are so familiar with.

On a warm summer's evening, I parked my cruiser under one of the large light poles at the Columbia Mall, where I intended to go over the last of the paperwork from the previous night's shift. I was there for only a few minutes when I saw a car stop by the Hecht

Company near the loading and unloading dock. I put the paperwork on the seat beside me when the driver pulled the car up in front of me and stopped.

A moment later he was asking, "Officer, is that a skunk?" as he pointed back in the direction of the ramp leading to the loading and unloading dock.

I glanced to my right and, sure enough, a very large skunk (all wildlife in and around Columbia lived the good life because of food disposed of in trash dumpsters) was at that moment waddling down the ramp. "Yes, sir, that's a skunk."

"We're all from the city, and none of us has ever seen a skunk before."

"Well, tonight's your lucky night."

With that he looked at me and, very seriously, said, "Are they friendly?"

Holy shit! A live one, I thought. "Yes, sir. Actually, the skunks in Columbia are tame and you can walk right up to one and pet him." Of course, I didn't really think that anyone was naïve enough to believe that.

"No shit!" he said, with a big grin on his face.

Now the game was on. *Is this guy really this gullible?* "Oh, yes, sir. You can drive over there, get outta your car and pet him."

"No shit!" he practically screamed.

"Yes, sir," I said, now thinking he couldn't possibly be that stupid.

With that, he turned and trotted back to his car yelling, "The officer said it's a skunk and it's tame. We can pet him."

Then, a moment later he was driving back toward the Hecht Company's loading dock and I was shaking my head, and wondering if they would actually get out of their car to try and pet the skunk. I had my answer almost immediately. The car stopped, four doors opened and six people exited. In an instant, they were scurrying, like excited school children on their first field trip, down the ramp.

"Son-of-a-bitch!" I blurted. "Those assholes are really gonna try and pet the skunk."

I put the car in gear and hauled ass off the lot. It was time to beat a very hasty path away from the mall. Why? Because, one very large cornered skunk, plus six gullible city slickers intent on petting him, equalled disaster of major proportions. That, of course, would probably add up to a complaint being lodged against the Howard County Police Officer who told them the skunks in Columbia were tame and could be petted. That is, if they could identify him.

I drove by the loading dock about an hour later and it reeked of "skunk perfume," but there were no signs of the skunk, or those daring city dwellers that came to Howard County in search of adventure. I guess that was all the adventure they could stand, because no one complained.

Caution: Skunk – Take Two

Howard County Police Officer Bob Smith in the lead role

While working evening shift on a Sunday, Bob Smith asked to go to Columbia, from his post on U. S. Route One, to conduct a follow up investigation. It was quiet at the time and I gave him the okay.

About an hour later, I received a call from him. "Can you meet me ASAP?"

The ASAP at the end of an officer's radio transmission usually meant that they had something important on their agenda. So, I headed up Route 32 to meet him near Hammond High School. As I was approaching his car, I noticed that all of the windows on his cruiser were open. I thought that rather odd, because there was a brisk chill in the air, but when I pulled in beside him I said, "Holy Jesus, Bob. What the hell did you do, hit a skunk?"

"No, Sarge, not exactly."

"Not exactly. What's that mean?"

"Uh, well, I took care of my follow up and I was on the way to my cruiser. I was rounding a corner to go to the parking lot and, the next thing I know, I'm face to face with a skunk."

I tried not to laugh. "Let me guess. A big skunk with wide white stripes down his back."

"Yes, sir, that's a good description. Anyway, I tried to back up, but I must've really pissed him off, because a second later he opened fire on me."

"Where'd you get hit?"

"Just my uniform pants."

After a little chuckle, I said, "You have any clean ones at the station?"

"No, sir. I'll hafta go home to change."

By now, it was late in the shift and it would've been a waste of time to have him go home, change clothes and came back to work. "Just go ahead and secure. Go home and clean up."

"Okay." He paused for a second. "Uh, Sarge, whatever do, please don't tell the guys what happened. You know, they'll never let me live it down."

"Bob, don't worry, I won't volunteer a thing," I said. Of course, that didn't mean I'd ignore a question.

By time the shift ended, everyone on the squad knew that Bob had secured early and gone home. And, it wasn't long before Ricky Lee raised the first question. "Sarge, what happened to Bob? He isn't sick, is he?"

"Not in the barfing sense, no."

"Sarge, you've got that look. What's up?"

I merely pointed out that Bob had had a very unfortunate encounter with a skunk in Columbia, and all hell broke loose. It was a certainty that the following afternoon, Bob would gain lots of support and words of encouragement over his misfortunate.

I was the first to meet Bob the next day, but I didn't stick him with a barb. I knew there'd be enough of those waiting when he went inside. He showed me the uniform pants he'd been wearing when he was "shot" by the skunk. There were white spots all over the front of the legs. The spray had actually bleached out the dark blue color of the pants.

I told him to take the pants to the Quartermaster's Office, along with a requisition for a new pair. I also told him that I was sure the Quartermaster would love to know how the pants were damaged, but there was still a rather distinct aroma about them.

Bob went inside, with me close behind, and moments later he received a "very warm welcome" from fellow squad members.

"Hey, Pepe."

"Officer LePew, great to have you back at work."

"Hey, Pepe, did your wife let you in the house last night?"

"What's more important—Pepe, did you get laid last night?"

"Only if his wife liked his new after shave."

Bob looked back at me. "Sarge, it hit me on the way home last night, that with your reputation, my ass was as good as cooked."

Police Officer Robert Smith would now have a nickname that would follow him for the rest of his days in the department, and an interesting tale to tell those who would ask how he got it.

Mrs. John B. Trotter

The Legend of Granny Trotter told by Jim Lilley

Mrs. John B. Trotter, or Granny as she was so affectionately called by many, was not a police officer, but every officer who met her loved her. I met Granny just prior to entering the police academy and, instantly, she became a heroine to me. She was a petite woman in her 80s, who spent almost every waking moment working in her yard.

When my brother-in-law, Angelo, saw her walking up the driveway, he said, "My God, she walks up that hill like she's nineteen."

She cut the grass, raked leaves, pruned shrubs, washed the windows, swept the stone patio every morning and painted the lawn furniture. When she wasn't working around the house, she was off somewhere helping someone else, or doing volunteer work at a church function. She was never idle.

I asked, one day, if she wanted my help with any of the chores. She gave me a quick smile and leaned her rake against a tree.

"Sonny, this is my life's pleasure. I take pride in my home

and yard and I feel a lot better because I keep it up."

Well, I couldn't argue with her logic.

Naturally, when she raked leaves, she also burned them. In those days there was a restriction on burning leaves, and a county ordnance stated that they could only be burned after 4:00 PM. It was late fall and about mid afternoon, and Granny had the leaf pile at full burn. As always, she had cleared a wide area around the burning leaves and dragged the lawn hose within easy reach. While the smoke swirled up through the now leafless Oak Trees, Officer Rogers was pulling into Granny's winding driveway.

"Mrs. Trotter, you know you can't burn leaves until after four o'clock."

"Is that so?"

"Yes, ma'am. It's a county law."

"Well, Sonny, by four o'clock my day's coming down to an end. I'm puttin' away the rake and hose and headin' into the house for a hot bath. Then it's suppertime and a little TV before bed. So, if you'd like to stop by after four o'clock and burn 'em, you can just do that."

According to Officer Rogers, it was hard not to laugh at her reply and even more difficult to try and scold Granny for burning leaves. "I liked her the moment I met her." Before leaving he said, "Well, Mrs. Trotter, you go ahead and burn the leaves. I really don't know anybody who's gonna arrest you for it."

I also discovered that Granny Trotter had a backbone that would make many a man envious. She went storming out of her kitchen door, over the stone wall by the driveway and into the woods after two men, who were armed with shotguns and hunting squirrels. By the time I ran down the stairs, she was escorting them out of the woods and, I assure you, that in her own polite way, she was tearing them a new ass. She sometimes gave permission to a select few to hunt on her property, but only if they obeyed her strict rules of sportsmanship. That being, they had to hunt at the very back edge of her land, because she considered the squirrels near her house to be her friends. And, indeed, she fed them everyday, along with the birds, rabbits and every now and then a raccoon. She was trusted enough by these creatures that a few took food from her hand. But, these two men very foolishly broke Granny's law and shot a squirrel behind the garage. Their permission to hunt was immediately and forever revoked.

Not long after I first met Granny, she called me into her kitchen, saying she wanted to show me something. She handed me a Harrington and Richardson shotgun. Well, in reality, it was a .410 gauge pistol, measuring a total of 12 inches in length, and having an eight-inch barrel. It was called an H&R Handy Gun. She said kept if for self-protection, but really had it more for "blasting snakes."

She told me she tucked it into her apron pocket when she worked in the yard in early spring and during the summer months. She confided, "Mind you, it's not that I'm afraid of snakes. I just don't like 'em. So, when I'm workin' out there in the yard and run across one, I just blast him." She told me that if I wanted to borrow it and test fire it to see how it handled, I was welcome to do so. I said that I'd certainly take her up on that offer.

It wasn't but a day or two later when I heard her calling me. I looked out the window from my apartment above and she said, "Come down here, quick."

I hurried out the door and down the stairs to find Granny standing near the back patio, holding her gun. She pointed down into the basement stairwell, where a garter snake lay coiled up near the water drain. She stuck the gun in my hand and said, "Go ahead and blast him."

The truth is, if I had seen the snake down there and Granny wasn't around, I would've picked it up and tossed it into the woods. But, she had me on the spot and I knew I couldn't disappoint her. I took the gun, drew the hammer back and aimed at the snake. A second later, I felt the recoil as I fired the gun and saw the snake fly backward into the wall.

"Well, how'd you like it?"

I looked back at her and Granny was beaming. I laughed. "That's quite a gun."

The following morning I looked out and saw Granny tucking

the gun into her apron pocket and dropping a few extra shells in behind it. She was off to work in the yard and rid the world of any unsuspecting reptile that happened to cross her path.

Some months later, perhaps even the following summer when my favorite call of all time, came over my police radio. As long as I live, I'll never forget the string of transmissions, which began with, "Headquarters to Unit 25."

"Twenty-five, Headquarters, go ahead."

"Unit 25, I have a Mrs. Trotter on the phone and she's asking if you could do her a favor."

"10-4, Headquarters, go ahead with the request."

"On your way home, she wants to know if you can stop by the hardware store and pick up a box of shotgun shells for her. She advises that she's running low on ammo and you know what she needs."

After I stopped laughing, I said, "10-4. Advise Mrs. Trotter I'll pick the shotgun shells up on my way home."

After I moved away, I often stopped by to say hello and see how she was doing. I usually found her working in the yard and, at just the right time of year, I could see the outline of the shotgun in her apron. I think she was close to 100 years of age when she passed on to the next life and I have a feeling she's probably giving advice on gardening and lawn care to Heaven's grounds keepers.

I've never forgotten Granny and she was my inspiration for a character in another book. With her attitude and courage, I imagine she could have worked in law enforcement, and I don't doubt for a moment that she would've served up an ass kicking to someone foolish enough to challenge her.

God Bless you, Granny, and thanks for the fond memories.

Reflections, Broken Glass and Startling Revelations

Howard Cogle recalls his days with the Baltimore City Police

There were several boarded up buildings on my foot post, and it was not unusual to find them forced open. Over time, I had discovered stolen property hidden in these abandoned buildings and was able to arrest a number of persons responsible for the thefts.

There was also an old movie house that had closed down and was boarded up, but I had not yet been inside. Eventually, I found some of the wooden panels had been removed, allowing access to the building. I went inside and saw that some old, tattered carpet was all that remained. It seemed odd to see a movie theater without the candy counter, hand railings and seats.

It was very dark and I was using my flashlight to find my way through the old building, when I heard a noise off to my left. It sounded as though someone had taken a few steps, and I paused and listened. I waited a few seconds and began moving in the direction where the noise had come from. Soon, I found myself outside what had once been the men's restroom.

I moved my light back and forth and stepped around the barrier, into the room. I looked to my right and then back to my left, again moving my light from side to side. An instant later, a beam of light was directed back at me and, now it sounded like footsteps moving toward me.

I drew my revolver and yelled, "Stop! I'm a police officer."

Instead of stopping, the footsteps sounded like they were moving closer. I fired twice and, at that exact moment, I saw two flashes, meaning someone was returning fire. I was sure I'd been shot, but I didn't feel any pain and, with a quick look, I didn't see any blood.

I spun my flashlight back to my left and noticed a mirror with two bullet holes.

Suddenly, I realized that I had opened fire on my reflection, but it didn't explain the sound of hurrying footsteps. That's when I was almost knocked over by two very large raccoons. They seemed to be in a big hurry to get out of the men's room, but it was a safe assumption that they didn't encounter a police officer who shot his reflection every day.

Now, I can't confess my "sins" without telling a quick story about my good friend, Lee Goldman. Lee and I worked together in Baltimore City before we moved on to the Howard County Police Department.

Lee had a number of abandoned and boarded up buildings on his post and, as fate would have it, he found one that had been broken open. Being the good officer that he was, he went inside to conduct a search. The place was a mess—broken chairs, tables, bottles and a few rats scurrying about to make life interesting.

Lee picked his way around the first floor and, not finding anybody, headed up the stairs to the second floor. Wouldn't you know it? The second floor was dirtier than the first floor. He said there were newspapers, magazines, broken bottles, beds, chairs and tables.

He went into one room and there was a table off to his right with a glass sitting on it. He was using his flashlight to look around the room and, when he glanced to his left, a pretty hefty gust of wind whipped the curtains up from the window back on his right. The curtain hit the glass, knocked it to the floor and it shattered.

Lee spun around quickly, and thought the waving curtain was someone running toward him. He pulled his revolver and opened fire, but missed the curtain and put six rounds in the wall of the empty building next door.

Potty Training

There was one thing in Baltimore City that indicated you were no longer a rookie, but a seasoned, veteran officer, and that was expertise in twirling your nightstick. Officers who were assigned foot posts wanted to become adept in the art of twirling the nightstick, because it showed those residing within your beat that you were not to be take lightly.

Of course, right out of the academy, I was assigned a foot post and I vowed that I would practice day and night, if necessary, to impress everyone on my beat and my fellow officers. Naturally, this meant that I'd be spending a great deal of off duty time honing my twirling skills.

I would stand in my living room and practice and I thought I was getting very good at twirling my nightstick. My wife, on the other hand, wasn't as impressed with my skills as I was, and decided to put her foot down. I really don't know why she was upset. I mean, I hadn't broken the television, or any windows or split a coffee table while I worked at building my proficiency. Now, I had knocked over three lamps, but in my defense, none of them broke. But, she overruled my defense and banished me to the bathroom. She said I could twirl my stick in there all day.

I couldn't believe that she had actually exiled me to the bathroom. I was sharpening my skills with a nightstick not being potty trained. In fact, I had already passed potty training. Anyway, there was no use arguing with her, so I trudged off to the bathroom to practice.

The bathroom in our house wasn't very wide. It was deep and narrow, but I had work to do. I began to twirl the stick with my right hand and I was doing quite well. I picked up the pace a little and was feeling rather comfortable. But, I also had to learn to twirl the stick with my left or weak hand, because true veterans were competent at using the nightstick with either hand.

I switched hands and started to twirl and, in no time at all, I was getting pretty comfortable with my ability. So, it was time to add some speed. There I was, spinning the stick faster and faster and feeling downright cocky. That's when the nightstick flew out of my hand, ricocheted off the tile wall, sailed back and glanced off the side of my head. I spun around trying to catch it, but only succeeded in knocking it into the opposite wall. It bounced off of that wall, hit my shoulder, went back and hit the wall again, fell to the floor and rebounded upward. I grabbed at it again, knocked it into the wall to my left, where it promptly shot back and hit me in the forearm. All of a sudden I felt like I was in a full-fledged deadly encounter with my nightstick, and it was kickin' my ass around the room. The only thing missing was movie or TV sound effects to heighten the drama. I don't know how many times I got hit before I finally got it under control, but I had welts on my arms, my legs and a nice goose egg on the side of my head.

My wife overheard the commotion and came running to the bathroom to see what the problem was. When I tried to explain, she burst into a fit of laughter but at the time, I didn't think it was that funny. On the bright side, though, I didn't have any injuries that required a trip to the hospital. I mean, how would I explain to the doctors and nurses the reason for the bumps and bruises? Then there would've been the embarrassment of them calling the department and saying, "Hey, we have one of your officers here who just got his ass kicked by his own nightstick."

Late Night Swim in Lake Elkhorn

Sergeant Jim Lilley and a U. S. Naval Academy Midshipman

Having been a Marine, it had always been my personal policy to extend every possible courtesy and break to members of the United States Military. The exceptions were those who were AWOL, or involved in a serious crime. Others received my "This is your lucky day" speech and were sent on their way.

I was working the night shift on a Friday in late May, and it was a warmer than usual night, but relatively quiet. Somewhere around 0100, a call was dispatched of a drowning in Lake Elkhorn. I arrived, along with several other officers, and a group of young men and women informed us that a friend tried to swim across the lake and had gone under. They said that they had been drinking when one member of their group said he could swim across the lake. Of course, his boast led to a few bets against him and, then the ultimate challenge—a dare. At that point, he stripped down to his shorts and dove in.

Members of the Howard County Fire Department had arrived and put a boat in the water to search for the young man. While they were searching, one of the young ladies told us that the man who had gone into the water was from the United States Naval Academy.

Almost at that very instant, someone called out from the lake that they had located the swimmer. Not only had they found him but also he was alive and well and apparently still swimming.

They managed to get him into the boat and bring him ashore, where he was told to gather his clothes and get dressed. It was quite obvious that he was drunk and I wondered how he had survived, because he had been in the water at least an hour before he was located. He was taken into custody, transported to the police station and placed in a cell.

The officer who had transported him to the station asked what he should charge him with. I laughed and said, "We won't file charges. We'll call the Naval Academy and let them take care of it. I'm sure whatever they do, will far surpass anything he'll get in court."

I called the Naval Academy, spoke with the Officer of the Day and told him what had happened. Then I went to the cell and informed the Midshipman that someone from the academy was on the way to pick him up.

He said, "Whatever you do, please don't tell me that prick, Major Garcia, is the Officer of the Day."

"Okay, I won't tell you that prick, Major Garcia, is the Officer of the Day."

"Thank God for that," he muttered and sat down on the bunk.

About an hour later a jeep pulled on to the back lot, with a Marine Lance Corporal driving and the Officer of the Day, Major Garcia, seated to his right. I saluted the Major as he stepped out of the jeep and understood why the young lad in the cell was scared shitless.

Major Garcia was a most impressive figure, standing at least 6'3" and appeared as advertised—a lean, mean, fighting machine. I smiled and imagined that many a new arrival at the U. S. Naval Academy damned near fainted the first time they saw him. And, judging by the way that the Midshipman in the cell wanted to avoid all contact with him, he must have instantly put the fear of God in their hearts and minds.

I escorted Major Garcia and his driver into the building and, a few moments later, we were standing in front of the detention cell.

In no time at all, the young man was on his feet and looking at me. "Sir, you... You told me Major Garcia wasn't the Officer of the Day."

I smiled. "No, that's not what I said. Remember, you said to me, 'Whatever you do, don't tell me that prick, Major Garcia, is the Officer of the Day.' And I said, 'Okay, I won't tell you that prick, Major Garcia, is the Officer of the Day.' So, I told you what you wanted to hear."

"Oh, God, I'm a dead man," he said, as I opened the cell. "I would've been better off if I just drowned."

When the jeep pulled off the lower lot, the Lance Corporal was grinning, Major Garcia was scowling and, it looked to me as if, the Midshipman was praying.

Flare Delivery

Lieutenant Howard Cogle and friends

I don't recall which of the hurricanes it was—Agnes or Eloise, but the aftermath was the same. The entire lower end of Main Street, Ellicott City had been flooded and a few of the buildings designated unsafe and some had been boarded up. Naturally, a number of the locals had to tear off the boards and go inside.

After one of the sweeps to clear the buildings, three of the Main Street regulars were brought into the station. Just about the time that they were brought into the station, I was called upstairs and told about the arrival of a flare delivery. I didn't think much of it until I looked outside and saw the truck.

We were already strapped for manpower, with officers being called in to work double shifts and some even working beyond a double. There were no officers in the building and I couldn't call any of them in off the street to help unload the truck. And I'm sure it would've taken me hours to unload the truck by myself. All of a sudden I had an idea.

I went downstairs and asked the officer with the three Main

Street boys if he'd processed them yet. When he said, "No" I said, "Good. Now, what I want you to do is bring them to me one at a time."

I hurried over to the Lieutenant's office and sat down behind the desk. Next, I called the officer and told him to bring one of the prisoners in. A few seconds later he had the first prisoner standing in front of the desk.

I looked up at the guy and said, "Due to the state emergency, you'll hafta stand trial right away."

The officer gave me a rather blank look, but the guy said, "Okay."

"You were brought in because you were found in one of the boarded up buildings on lower Main Street, is that right?"

"Yes, sir."

"Okay. I find you guilty of trespassing. But, in my court, you have a choice of punishment. You can help unload flares and stack them here in the building, or you can go to jail. If you unload flares, you'll be released after the job's finished."

"Uh, I'll unload flares."

"Good. Have a seat in the outer room and I'll be with you in a few minutes." When he went out into the briefing room and sat down, I told the officer to bring the next one in. He laughed and went to fetch the next prisoner.

In record time I had convicted three men of trespassing and sentenced them to unload flares. Then I marched them up to the truck, where I supervised the unloading and, true to my word, released them when the job was completed.

This Is a Test

I was working the night shift and, part of my job during that tour was reviewing reports submitted by the day and evening shifts.

The Howard County Police Reporting System at that time consisted of the Short Form and Long Form Reports. The short forms were for reporting minor incidents and the long forms for reporting serious crimes. There were always a number of minor faults that seemed to crop up, such as forgetting to include someone's date of birth, or leaving some of the boxes blank.

One night I was reviewing a short form report that had been submitted by Officer Don Cook and approved by, then, Corporal James Lilley. It appeared to be nothing out of the ordinary, just a burglar alarm at the Bugatch Furniture Company at the Columbia Mall. As long as the alarm was accidental or a false alarm, it was permissible to write it up on the short form. But, in this case, the fact that it had a notation, "continued on side two" raised my curiosity. I turned the report over and read, "After my initial response to Bugatch Furniture, I decided to return and speak with the representative again. At that time I discovered that Miss French was not an employee of the company and had actually been the lookout for a team of burglars. The thieves made off with $250,000 worth of furniture before store employees arrived for work. No further action taken."

Well, I went right through the roof, but I should've known something was out of place. I couldn't understand why Corporal Lilley, of all supervisors, would've approved such a report. If anyone knew what the proper procedures were for such crimes, he did. If nothing else, I thought he would've taken Don Cook outside and stuffed him in the dumpster for failing to notify him and call out criminal investigators and the crime lab.

When Sergeant Mike Chiuchiolo arrived for work in the morning, I called him in and went over the report with him. He was so riled up over the report and failure to follow procedure, I thought I'd hafta get him a tranquilizer to calm him down. About a minute later, Corporal Lilley and Officer Cook walked into the building where they were greeted by both of us. Well, they started laughing and I knew something was up.

Don Cook said, "I wondered if anybody upstairs actually read the reports before they were filed. So, after I handled the alarm at Bugatch, I wrote up the two reports. At the end of the shift, I went to Corporal Lilley, showed him both reports and asked if we should run a test to see if anyone read them. He went along with it, but said, 'If Sergeant Cogle's working tonight, I'd bet he reads every last one of them.' And, we found out, you do."

After Lilley and Cook had their asses chewed, Don gave me the original report and I was happy. As for Mike, I think it might've taken him a few days to cool down.

Round Up Time

One thing I learned in a hurry after leaving Baltimore City and coming to Howard County was, loose animal calls were not uncommon. From horses to cows, to sheep and goats, I listened to the calls dispatched, or responded to help chase them down.

A young man by the name of Tommy Watkins had just graduated from the academy and was in his field-training phase. Tommy was working the night shift with our squad and, as it happened that particular night, he was riding with me.

We were dispatched to check a location for loose horses almost immediately after calling in service. I told him we'd have to approach cautiously so we wouldn't spook the horses and, while we were looking for the horses, we would also hafta look for a ruptured fence.

We arrived in the area where the horses were last seen, and I noticed Tommy looking around, turning his head anxiously from side to side. I asked if something was wrong.

"I'm looking for this ruptured fence, but since I don't know a lot about horses, I have no idea what the hell a ruptured fence is."

Naturally, I laughed. "It's a fence with a hole in it." You know, he didn't laugh at my answer. I don't think he thought it was funny.

A minute or two later, we spotted the horses and, as we approached, two of them went back through the hole in the fence and into the field. The third one though was apparently enjoying his freedom a little too much and went on down the road. So, here we are pursing a horse in a police car and Tommy wanted to know how we were gonna catch it.

"Well, lights and siren are outta the question. I don't think he's gonna pull over to the side of the road, stop and, surrender if I turn 'em on."

But, at that very moment, a daring idea came to mind. Well, the daring part was actually gonna be Tommy's.

"Quick, get on your knees on the seat, lean out the window and when I drive up next to the horse, you reach out and grab him."

Now, a veteran officer would've told me to go screw myself, but Tommy, being a fresh recruit, followed my command to the letter. In no time at all, he's on his knees on the seat and hanging out the window.

We're now in hot pursuit and gaining on the horse, and Tommy's hanging out the window and stretching as far as he can, trying to grab the horse. I eased the car a little closer and he managed to grab him. Well, the natural reaction of the horse was to try and escape.

The horse turns to his right and Tommy's going out the window. I reached over and grabbed his gun belt with my right hand, while continuing to drive beside the horse. I'm not sure how many times he almost went out the window, but it had to be close to six times. Finally, somehow—don't ask me how, we actually managed to apprehend the horse with this "daring" maneuver.

Taking him to the station, photographing and hoof printing him was out of the question. Besides, I don't think he would've fit in the back of the car and we didn't have a prisoner van.

We did get him back into the pasture and the owner of the horses came out and repaired the fence. The rest of the night was relatively calm and I don't think Tommy really cared.

Happy Halloween

P.F.C. James "J. D." Dawson, Grand Prize Winner

It was in the early 70s and, as Halloween approached, it seemed like the perfect excuse for a party. Not that members of the Howard County Police Department needed a special occasion to party in those days. Then came the idea of a costume party and, suddenly, there was an almost overwhelming air of enthusiasm running through the ranks. Throw in a prize for the best, or most original costume, which added a challenge and it brought out the thinking caps.

About two weeks before the party, Jimmy Dawson said he had a great idea for a costume. When he said it, he laughed and I wondered what he had in mind. So, I asked what he was coming as.

"A dildo."

"Yeah, J. D., right."

"I'm serious," he replied, without cracking a hint of a smile.

Late afternoon, on the day of the party, J. D. knocked at my door and asked if I could help bring his costume to the house. I noticed that he was driving Don Bathgate's pickup truck and I was sure he was screwing with me. But, he insisted that he needed help loading his costume, getting it to my house and hiding it in the garage until the right time to make his entry.

I knew he had taken off for the party, but he had everyone convinced that he was working night shift, because his leave had been refused. I must admit that I was getting more than just a little curious about what he was up to. So, a minute later I was in the truck and headed to "The Mansion" where he said his costume was in the basement.

Well, I followed J. D. down the outside steps and into the basement.

When he flipped on the lights and I saw his costume, I lost it. There, just as he'd promised, was a perfect replica of a penis. It was constructed using chicken wire, wrapping layers of thin plastic wrap and spray-painting it. The shaft was painted beige, but he'd made a masterpiece of the head and had spray painted it bright red.

J. D. wasn't five feet tall. He is closer to six feet and, even though he wasn't a body builder, his work of art was over six feet in height and the circumference had to be substantial enough to encase his entire body—no armholes allowed he said.

We loaded it into the back of the truck and, in no time at all, we were southbound on U. S. Route 29.

It was the beginning of the evening rush hour and suddenly a horn was sounding from behind us. I looked back and saw the penis rising from the bed of the truck and, yes, the head was pointed directly at the car to our rear. The car was occupied by at least five people, all of whom were pointing and laughing. Soon, it seemed like we were leading a parade down Route 29. There were flashing lights, honking horns and countless pointing fingers and our "lead float" was the center of attention.

I turned to J. D. "I think we'd better pull over and weight your costume down with something. It's rising up in the back of the truck and giving quite a thrill to all the homeward bound workers."

J. D. took a quick look over his right shoulder and slowed

down. The costume immediately began to sink back into the bed. Then, he accelerated and, sure enough, it started to rise again. Well, that was all it took for J. D. to decide it was time to really entertain the hard working public. For the next mile he sped up and slowed down, allowing the penis to rise and fall and "flash" the weary workers. Although, I think this might have been the highlight of their workday, if not their workweek.

J. D. laughed. "You know, I bet this is the first time they ever saw a pickup truck with a hard-on."

When we exited Route 29 on to Route 40, I thought we were headed to my house off St. John's Lane. J. D. had other ideas. He wanted a sandwich and drove direct to the Village Green Shopping Center. When we got out of the truck a woman was walking by carrying a little boy.

The little boy pointed into the bed of the truck and said, "Mommy, what's that?"

She turned her head and looked. "That's... Oh, My God!" She turned a nice deep shade of red and hurried on by.

It was close to midnight when J. D. made his grand entrance into the party and, he was an instant hit. By now everyone had gotten into the spirit with the help, of course, of plenty of free flowing spirits and the giant penis was an instant hit. Several women ran to greet the beige and red monster, one throwing her arms around it and declaring, "Where have you been all my life?"

Then the guessing game began. Who was hiding behind that most magnificent costume? The first name mentioned was Frank Becker, because everyone seemed to agree that if anyone would dare appear as a dildo, it would be Frank. After "closer study" it was decided that it couldn't be Frank, because the girth wasn't wide enough.

After nearly 45 minutes of suspense, J. D. slipped off the costume and received a round of applause for his creative genius. Needless to say, he won the bottle of Seagram's 7.

When the party ended, J. D. left his costume in my garage, saying he would return in a day or two to retrieve it.

There is another tale attached to this creation, which I've sworn I had nothing to do with. Yet, it seems that most refuse to believe that I was on vacation at the time of the event and out of town.

It seems that "monster pecker" somehow made its way out of my garage, which by the way couldn't be locked, and was stuffed into a telephone booth at St. John's Plaza. Next, an anonymous call was made to the Waterloo State Police Barrack, the caller telling MSP that no county officers were available to respond to a call. Within minutes a trooper was dispatched to a report of a "suspicious looking subject" in a phone booth.

After all parties involved, including the trooper, enjoyed a good laugh, the penis found its way back to my garage.

When talk began circulating that the penis was going to be taken to the Enchanted Forest and attached to the statue of Old King Cole, I knew it was time to put it "to rest."

Howard County Adventures with Roger Neubauer

Sadly, Roger passed away in 2004, but those of us who remember him so well, know this work would be incomplete without including some of his stories.

The Search Warrant Wait

It was one of those hurry up and wait cases, and those of us waiting to carry out the raid were packed like sardines into the criminal investigations office. A group that included Bob Mathews, Jack Burke, Mike Chiuchiolo and Jim Robey were gathered around a desk playing cards. A few others were reading, working on reports, or follow up investigations.

Roger and I, however, found some unusual entertainment using the 20 pound sledgehammer, which was to be used to "knock" on the door of the home to be raided, a tennis ball and a Styrofoam coffee cup. Although neither of us engaged in the game of golf, we invented a new version of the sport using the "door key" to knock the tennis ball into the cup.

Roger immediately dubbed the event "The Spiro Agnew Open" and the game began with him "sinking" his first putt. Soon, he was lining up, looking to me and saying, "Signal the gallery for quiet." The gallery being those engaged in the poker game.

I would turn, render a single finger gesture to the group, and announce, "Sir, the gallery has been signalled."

After an hour or so of "golf" the challenge was wearing off and Roger quietly said, "A cold beer would sure hit the spot."

"Roger, it's not like we can just walk outta here, go for a cold one and stop back like nothing's happened. We're supposed to go on this raid."

"Yeah, but we're the odd men out. We're just along for extra numbers and, what the hell, one won't hurt us."

"Yeah, I know that," I said, wondering what he had in mind. "But, we can't walk over to the boss and say, 'Goin' out for a beer. Be right back.'"

He sat down at his desk, as though lost in deep thought. A few minutes later he sprang to his feet and blurted. "Son-of-a-bitch!"

I believe it was Jack Burke who looked at him and said, "Roger, are you okay?"

"No. Damn, I can't believe I forgot to buy toothpaste."

"Buy toothpaste?"

"My mother's almost outta toothpaste and I told her I'd pick up a tube on my way to work. She's probably completely out by now." He grabbed his jacket and headed for the door. "I'll run up to the pharmacy at the Golden Triangle and buy a tube. Be right back." He then turned to me. "Come on, Jim, ride up with me."

"What if the go ahead call comes in while you're out?" Burke said.

"Don't worry, Boss, we'll have a portable radio," he called over his shoulder as he charged out the door with me on his heels.

About two minutes later we were seated at the bar in Buell's

Restaurant on the corner of Route 40 and Rogers Avenue, with a cold bottle of Budweiser. Of course, I guess it looked strange to patrons seeing, what was obviously some type or radio, sitting between the bottles. And, sure enough, one of them, who was not a regular, had to ask what it was for.

Roger didn't miss a beat. "We're monitoring traffic at the airport for suspicious flights from Albania."

"Oh," was the only reply, but there were more than a few choked guffaws from those who knew us.

We finished our beer and, as we headed to the car, Roger said, "Guess we'd better get back to the station."

Although I had a feeling that Jack Burke probably suspected our real reason for our hurried departure, I said, "You might wanna get a tube of toothpaste before we go back. Just in case the boss asks to see what you bought."

"Yeah, good idea."

We drove to the pharmacy at the Golden Triangle and went straight to the oral hygiene aisle. That's when Roger proved he wasn't making an extra effort to cover the beer run. He grabbed the smallest tube of Crest Toothpaste on the shelf, which I believe was only a little more than a half-ounce in content and probably cost about 39 cents.

"Don't you think you should buy a bigger tube?"

"Nah. I'll just say mom has small teeth."

Back at the station Jack shot us a rather curious glance, but never said a word. And, an hour or so later, the raid went off without a hitch.

The Fresh Scent of Tobacco

For reasons unknown to his co-workers, Roger decided to take up smoking a pipe. Granted, Roger was a long time smoker, but seeing him walking around, or sitting with his feet propped up on his desk, puffing at the pipe seemed almost comical.

At the time, he was in his late twenties, and fellow detectives thought the pipe was more suited to older gentlemen. On the other hand, he was also very slender, or more appropriately, down right skinny is probably a better description. Very quickly it became a standing joke within the division that he could hide behind his pipe stem.

In those days, there was no such thing as a "Smoke Free" building and Roger was having a very difficult time selecting a satisfactory brand of pipe tobacco. So, it was almost a daily routine that members of the division were treated to a new aroma while he searched for his favorite taste. Of course, the office space housing the division was very small at the time, and it didn't take long to over power the room with the fragrance of the day.

There were growing complaints over his pipe smoking, which grew more vocal when it was discovered that he was only smoking the pipe at work and inside the office. Pleas, asking him to show a little compassion and smoke the pipe outside were ignored. He argued that it was too cold to smoke outside, which meant it was also too cold to open the office windows and allow in a breath of fresh air.

Weeks went by and the grumbling continued over his pipe habit, and threats were being made that his pipe or tobacco can was going to be filled with cow or horse manure. Hand written notes and signs were taped to his desk declaring the area as unsafe, a firetrap and public health menace, but Roger would not give up his pipe.

In the afternoons, there was always overlap time between the day and evening shifts, and by 4:00 PM almost every member of the division was crammed into the office.

It was one of those packed house days when Roger arrived, sat down at his desk and reached for his pipe. A few detectives noticed a puzzled look on his face when he picked up the pipe, but he shrugged and leaned back in his chair. A chorus of groans filled the room when he opened the matchbook, took out a match, and touched a flame to the tobacco. He propped his feet up on his desk and puffed away, smiling as his pipe smoke filled the room.

Although everyone was making an effort to ignore him, first one detective, then another raised their heads and looked at him.

Soon, everyone was looking around and casting some very, very questioning glances in Roger's direction.

Sergeant Jack Burke, the division commander, and Corporal Michael Chiuchiolo, the assistant division commander, abruptly stopped talking and stared at Roger. In a matter of seconds they were glancing from one detective to another, both obviously bewildered by the aroma that was filling the air. By now, every detective in the room—every detective that is, except Roger, had recognized the very familiar odor of burning marijuana.

The look on the faces of everyone was asking the same question. "Who is the dumb shit smoking marijuana in the CID Squad Room?"

Of course, since Roger was the only one in the midst of those assembled currently smoking, it was rather easy to narrow the list of suspects. Yet, nobody in the room said a word to him, but turned instead to look at Jack Burke and Mike Chiuchiolo. After all, they were the commanders, and certainly it was their responsibility to call Roger on the carpet and put a stop to his clear-cut violation of the law. But, in spite of the reality of the situation and overwhelming evidence, no one wanted to believe that he was actually brazen enough to smoke grass in the police station.

Finally, Roger sat up in his chair, stared at his pipe and grumbled something about the terrible taste of the tobacco. He bolted out the door, appearing a few minutes later as if nothing had happened, and sat down at his desk. He grabbed a report, picked up the phone and called someone to discuss a burglary at their home.

Nobody ever stepped up and took credit for loading his pipe with marijuana. It was, however, a topic that came up from time to time over a cold beer, along with suspicions and speculation as to the identify of the culprit or culprits that "loaded" his pipe. Still, "the great stationhouse marijuana caper" held one very positive outcome. Roger never again smoked a pipe.

Holding all the Aces

The Rouse Company provided condominiums or apartments to its corporate representatives when they were visiting or working in Columbia, Maryland. They were furnished with all conveniences, including the latest in color televisions. As time passed, however, this tempting information reached the ears of certain would be entrepreneurs, who decided the easy way to open a "business" was with TVs provided by Rouse and Company.

Sometime on a Friday night, they broke into 19 or 20 of the residences and toted off the color televisions.

Bright and early the following Saturday morning, Detectives Jim Robey and Paul Hajek found themselves processing the crime scenes and searching for evidence in the cases. In no time at all, good detective work led to the name of a suspect, but try as they might, they couldn't piece together enough evidence to arrest him or obtain a search and seizure warrant for his apartment. Although they worked throughout the day, hoping to find that one elusive clue, the day ended in frustration.

Late that night, Jim and Paul were working a stakeout at the Columbia Exxon Station on Little Patuxent Parkway due to a rash of burglaries and thefts. They were still grumbling about their failure to close out the great TV heist, when Roger Neubauer drove up, parked his car and knocked at their door. When they opened the door, he casually strolled in with a six-pack of Budweiser under his arm.

Soon, he was listening to their tale of woe and how they just couldn't seem to piece together enough evidence to confront the suspect. Suddenly he had an idea. "Hey, you guys drive over to the area of his apartment and I'll get him to bring a TV out to you."

At first, they were sceptical, but when Roger put his plan on the table, they agreed that it might work. A few minutes later they were hiding in the area of the Dumpster near the suspect's apartment and waiting for Roger to do his part.

Later, Roger said, "I popped the top on a can of Bud, lit up a cigarette and sat down at the desk. I called the suspect and after a few rings he answered the phone. That's when I said 'Listen, pal, I know what you did last night and I want one of the televisions. And if you don't give me one of the TVs, I'm callin' the cops and rattin' your ass out.' He said he didn't know what I was talking about and that's when I told him exactly what he did. To prove it, I described the locations of the break-ins, how he got in, and gave him a perfect description of the televisions."

He hesitated for a few seconds and then said, "Okay, you got me. I don't know how, but you got me."

"That's right and don't forget it."

"Okay," he grumbled. "Okay, just tell me what you want."

"I know some of those TVs were brand new. So, I want one of them and there better not be any scratches on it."

Now the guy sounded a little pissed off. "Okay. Okay.

Christ, you're holdin' all the aces."

"Yeah. And, I got the Trump Card, too." I don't know what the hell that meant. I heard it somewhere and it sounded good, so I threw it in. Then I said, "Oh, by the way, it's startin' to rain. Make sure my TV's wrapped in something to keep it nice and dry."

"Okay. But, where do you want me to bring it?"

"I'll be outside in ten minutes. Meet me by the Dumpster."

As instructed, the suspect walked out of his apartment, with a television that was neatly covered with plastic wrapping, and into the waiting arms of Jim Robey and Paul Hajek. And, after his arrest, all stolen property was recovered.

At the police station, the suspect asked how Robey and Hajek knew he had been responsible for the break-ins and thefts. They said they received information from an informant and, naturally, he asked the name of the informant.

Those were the days when made up and outrageous fictitious names were a part of our every day and, in an instant, someone said, "Tillie Tooltaster."

"Tillie Tooltaster? Who the hell is Tillie Tooltaster?"

Roger, being in top form, said, "She's a full blooded Lumbee Indian who's had her VD card revoked."

Oddly, the suspect immediately thought he knew who she

was. "Damn, I bet it's that ugly broad I picked up and screwed last week, but I can't remember her name."

"It's probably her," Robey answered.

When the case went to the Circuit Court of Howard County for trial, the suspect's defense attorney cried entrapment. However, Chief Judge James MacGill ruled that he believed it to be excellent police work, and the defendant was found guilty.

Let's Surprise the Boss

It was Sunday and the evening shift in CID was coming to a close. Roger had some fireworks he'd found and was desperate to test them. This particular firework was designed with a string protruding from each end, which had to be attached to an object and pulled in order to detonate it. To test the device, he tied one end to the leg of his chair and the other to the leg of his desk. With a quick tug, he was treated to a loud bang, which he seemed to thoroughly enjoy.

The wheels were turning fast, and he wouldn't be satisfied unless we rigged a desk as a good morning surprise for some poor unsuspecting dayshift detective. Well, one thing leg to another and CID Commander, Jack Burke, was nominated for a wake up bang. But, Roger thought it should be something spectacular and taped three or four of the devices together.

Soon, we were both on the floor, working to attach the "bomb" to the boss' desk and chair. It took a little extra time and effort, because the strings also had to be twined together to ensure that the device worked properly. But, after a few minutes of "genius" cooperation, we turned out the lights and left for home.

The following morning, Roger had to return for court and destiny ruled that he should meet Jack Burke at George's Sub and Sandwich Shop while picking up a coffee. A few minutes later they were walking into the CID office together, and karma dictated that Roger should forget all about what he had taken part in the previous evening.

Jack went to his desk and Roger to his. Jack put his coffee down and pulled his chair out at the very moment Roger was taking the lid off his coffee cup. There was a loud explosion, followed by Roger screaming "son-of-a-bitch" and throwing his coffee over his desk and up the wall beside him. Jack yelled, "No good cocksucker" while he tried to wave the cloud of smoke away from his desk.

When I arrived for work that afternoon, I discovered that sole responsibility for the "bombing" was laid at my feet. Roger quickly pointed out that I was the Boss's first and only suspect, and he didn't want to take anything away from my reputation by confessing to a conspiracy. Fortunately, "The Boss" took the morning explosion as a prank and had a good laugh over it. After all, it seemed that Roger got the worst it.

Harvest Time

With ample spring rain and a burst of sunshine throughout late April and well into May, it was a great growing season. Calls had been received, reporting green leafy plants sprouting up in unusual locations around Howard County. Of course, that could mean only one thing. Young, brilliant, business minds, with visions of untold wealth pouring in, had planted their marijuana early.

Roger and I had been sent out to search the areas and, sure enough, we discovered a half-dozen locations where the plants were in various stages of growth. Some of the agricultural geniuses had gone to great lengths to conceal their crops from police and rival "business owners." One had staked out a sizeable "garden" in a wooden area off a rural county road. He then had to cut down dozens of trees, dig up the stumps and work the ground before planting his crop. Stashed under a tree was an array of fish and other fertilizers, along with gallons of water. Another had chosen an area in a large field about a half-mile from a high school. This particular "farm" was near a stream, which supplied water for his crop. Yet, another, located near Atholton Village, looked as though it was a "joint" venture. There were between 400 and 500 plants, which they attempted to conceal by planting them near hundreds of pine trees. As cleaver as they were at hiding their plants, they continually used the same path to check on and tend their crop.

In those days we lacked the manpower to cover a long-term stakeout to catch the culprits. We could only hope to apprehend them, with the luck of a chance encounter, while checking on the progress of their farms. We did our best to spot check the areas at least once a week, altering our days and times to avoid a pattern. But, we were never fortunate enough to walk up on the farmers while they were tending their crops.

Finally, Jack Burke said it was time for us to just go out and harvest the crops and bring them in to be destroyed. Naturally, Roger and I drew the assignment, but also back in those days, the police department didn't have a truck for our use. So, it was off to the harvest in an unmarked car.

Our first stop was by the streambed, where we pulled up 60 plants and stuck them in the trunk of the car. Next, came the crop in the woods, which yielded just over 100 plants. Before we left that location, we poured out all of his liquid fertilizer and water. Then it was on to a few other spots before heading to the "big one" behind Atholton Village. By the time we reached that location the trunk was filled to capacity. In fact, after our last stop we thought we would have to sit on the truck lid to close it.

We slipped into the field behind Atholton via a side street and parked our car. As we ripped up the plants, we carried them to the car and dropped them on the back floor of the car. Soon, the plants were piled on the seat and still rising. By the time that particular harvest was over, marijuana plants were sticking out the windows on both sides of the car.

We hit U. S. Route 29, northbound, around mid to late afternoon and immediately it seemed we were the center of attention. I could only imagine a State Police Narc or a Federal Agent driving up beside us, spotting our "marijuana wagon" and thinking he'd landed the easiest bust of his career. But, no narcs appeared and, strangely, no one called the police to report a mobile stash on Route 29.

Now, please don't think that Roger and I harvested these plants without leaving a little something behind for the hard working farmer. As I have confessed to on dozens of occasions, I can draw one thing and one thing only—one hell of an obscene gesture. So, each of the horticulturists was awarded a "finger" for his or her hard work. Of course, the bigger the crop, the larger and more colorful the gesture. Naturally, the grand prize winner was the Atholton

Village Farm, which was given a gesture, drawn on six pieces of 18 inch by 24 inch paper that had been carefully taped together. This "award" was planted squarely in the middle of their entranceway with the message, "Hey, Assholes, you've been ripped off."

A few days later, Jim Robey and I made it a point to stop by the Atholton Center. There were a few young gentlemen, all of whom we suspected were connected to the marijuana plants. They were standing around and looking very unhappy. Jim asked if everything was okay and the reply from them was, "There're some real common bastards around here."

Piggy Ham-let's One Night-Stand

Roger was a sergeant and Platoon Commander of the 5th Platoon and I was a corporal and squad leader of the Columbia Squad. There were only two days remaining of our night shift rotation, when John Langenfelder and Larry Freer came to me and said they had a great item to use for a little joke.

I followed them to the parking lot, where John pulled a dead piglet from the trunk of his car. John's uncle, who owned a farm in Clarksville, called and asked him to stop by on his way in to work. When John arrived, his uncle said he knew of our reputation as practical jokers and gave him the piglet, figuring that at least one of us would come up with an idea for a prank. He also told John that the animal had died earlier in the day and it was just one of those things that happened. Not all animals born on the farm survived.

The piglet probably weighed between 15 and 20 pounds. The mouth was opened just enough to show a row of sparking white teeth and, the way the lip curled, the damn thing looked like it had a smile on its face. And, in no time at all, we knew where Piggy Ham-let was going. Shortly after 0200 hours, Little Piggy was handcuffed with plastic Flex-cuffs to the front of Don Lundin's personal car.

At that time, Johnny Walker was the morning DJ at Radio Station WFBR in Baltimore, and was always ready for any new material he could sneak into his show or even the news. At 6:00 AM he went on the air with the morning news.

His very first announcement was: "This just in from my reliable source in Howard County. There's a pig handcuffed to

Officer Don Lundin's car. Well, Don, I hope that's not indicative of the type of women you like to date."

Don immediately drove to the lower lot of the police station to see if Johnny Walker's News broadcast was true. When he saw "Little Ham-let" grinning up at him, he jumped into the fun. He called over his radio and asked if someone could stop by and pick up eggs and bread on their way to the station.

Roger, who had also heard the news, made it to the parking lot in time to see Don cutting the cuffs and taking Ham-let off of his car. Of course, Piggy Ham-let made several other stops, including the car of a female police recruit, before ending up once again with John Langenfelder and Larry Freer for a proper burial. At the time, Roger had a good laugh, as did everyone else on the platoon. The bomb would drop later that morning.

When I arrived for work that night, Roger called me into his office and told me that he'd been ordered to conduct an investigation into the incident. Of course, I was the prime target of the inquiry and the powers at the top were more than a little upset over what had happened. That's when things got very ugly.

Apparently, someone who had heard Johnny Walker's News broadcast had a very overactive imagination. This person had placed a call to Howard County Executive, Hugh Nichols, and told him I had shot the pig simply to play a practical joke.

For a few moments, I thought this was only a prank being organized by Jim Robey and a few others. But, Roger said it was not a prank and he was also very concerned that this would end his chances of being promoted to lieutenant and mine for sergeant. Then, I knew he was serious.

Of course, the accusation that I shot the pig was quickly resolved with a telephone call to John Langenfelder's uncle. Then, Roger said, "Please tell me you didn't make the call to Johnny Walker at WFBR."

"I did call Johnny Walker."

"Damn it, Jim, I told you not to tell me that."

"Roger, I know you told me not to tell you that, but I'm not gonna lie about it. I called and I wouldn't expect Johnny Walker to lie about it if you asked him."

Roger got up and paced around the room, probably picturing his gold lieutenant's bars attached to the pig's ass. When he stopped pacing he said, "I don't even know what to put in the subject line of my report."

"How about Hogicide?" I said.

Through bursts of laughter he said, "Damn it, I'm trying to be serious."

"So, am I."

He completed his report and turned it over to Captain Jim Robey early the next morning. Jim took the findings to Colonel Paul Rappaport and, although not completely happy with the events, he was satisfied that the piglet had not been shot for the purpose of a practical joke. However, all was forgiven a few days later.

While the 5th Platoon was on a three-day break, a rape had occurred in the vicinity of the Columbia Mall. Detectives had very little to go on, and everyone was under a lot of pressure to locate and arrest the suspect. Investigators had interviewed dozens of people in and around the mall, but were unable to develop leads in the case.

Jim Robey called Roger and told him he wanted our squad to conduct another follow up investigation in the mall itself. So, Larry Freer, John Langenfelder and I began a store-to-store canvass, and talked with employees and customers alike. Within 30 minutes we had the suspect's name and home address. He was arrested later that afternoon, we were absolved of our sins and Piggy Ham-let became just another of those legendary police pranks.

When promotions were announced in November, Roger received his lieutenant's bars and I, my sergeant's stripes.

Wrong Number – Take One

An unknown caller and members of the Criminal

Investigations Division

We had a telephone in the CID office that was installed for the purpose of having informants call without having to go through the county or police switchboard. As could be expected, there were always calls coming in, day and night, where the calling party had dialled a wrong number. Calls came in asking for fuel oil deliveries, for clothing stores, restaurant reservations, and residences.

One particular Friday afternoon, someone began calling and asking for a woman by name. For this story, I'll call her Sadie. The detective that took the initial call told him, very politely, that he'd dialled a wrong number. About 15 minutes later the phone rang again, and it was the same man asking for Sadie. He was told that he'd called a wrong number.

Well, he obviously couldn't understand that the number he was dialling was incorrect. Soon, call after call was coming in and, each time now, a different detective answered the phone. Yet, no matter how polite the explanation, the man persisted in calling again and again.

I had not answered the phone, but I was getting more than a little annoyed by the calls. When the phone rang again, I jumped up from my desk and hurried to answer it.

I said, "Hello" and immediately the man asked for Sadie. With that I said, "Sorry, she can't come to the phone right now. She's upstairs fuckin' a few of the boys." Then, I hung up.

Needless to say, everyone in the room damn near fell out of their chairs—some laughing, others shocked by what I had told him.

"Well, get ready," I said. "In a few minutes we'll probably be responding to a homicide."

No calls were received reporting a murder, but the man never called back.

Wrong Number – Take Two

Jim and Mom

In my early days with the department, I hated taking the phone off the hook to avoid being ripped from a sound sleep. I didn't want to miss a possible call relating to a family or police department emergency.

There came a day when I had been to court after working all night and when I, at last, reached home all I wanted was a very, very peaceful sleep. It didn't take long for me to fall sound asleep, but the inevitable happened. The telephone rang and jolted me out of a rock solid sleep.

I somehow got out a very groggy "hello" and it sounded like the guy asked if this was a car repair shop. I told him "no" hung up, and stumbled back to bed. As soon as I drifted off, the phone was ringing again. So, back to the phone and the same guy who had just called. I told him it wasn't a car repair shop and he had a wrong number.

Naturally, this was an asshole that couldn't understand, after two messages, that he was calling a wrong number. I took his third call and responded with a message that was a bit more blunt than the previous two. I hung up and hadn't even made it back to bed, when the phone started ringing again. That was it.

I grabbed the phone and yelled, "You ignorant, no good mutha fucker. If you call me again, I'm gonna hunt your fuckin' ass down, shove your phone up your ass, rip out your fuckin' heart and feed it to my dog." I slammed the phone down and went back to bed, but now I was wide awake, which pissed me off even more.

Three or four days later, my mother called and invited me over to dinner. After a nice dinner and over a cold beer, she said, "I tried to call you a few days ago, but I sure must've dialled a wrong number. I got some man on the phone and, right away, he started cussing at me. I've never heard language like that in my life. He said he was gonna shove the phone—well, never mind where he was gonna shove it. But, his language was terrible."

Oh, Shit! She was the fourth caller! I thought. *I unloaded on Mom. Well, it sounded like she didn't recognize my voice.* So, I tried to cover my ass. "Mom, there are people out there like that. You just hafta take the good with the bad." Of course, I was hoping and praying that she wouldn't find out I was the bad one that day. But, I wasn't going to confess either.

You can't write Me a Ticket

Jim Lilley, 19 other officers and one idiot driver

It was the end of an evening shift and time for a cold beer. We went to our usual "Choir Practice" location, a dead-end street next to O'Donnell Pontiac in Ellicott City.

One of our dispatchers had picked up the beer and ice and, after uniform shirts were taken off and dropped into our cars, the first cold one of the night was opened.

We were standing around, talking about the day's calls and, of course, there were a few barbs flying around. The good-natured verbal jabs were as much a part of "Choir Practice" as the beer drinking. About a half-hour after our arrival, a car passed by the street, but suddenly the driver braked to a stop and backed up.

I guess he was curious as to what was going on, and he drove slowly down the street toward us. As he drove by, he and his two passengers stared at us and realized that we were police officers standing by the roadside and drinking beer. He made a U-turn, pulled up beside us and stopped. He and his friends started laughing, while he revved the engine of his Chevelle SS 396. A second later, he gunned it and began squealing wheels, still looking over at us.

With tires smoking, he roared up to the Stop Sign, went on through without stopping, and began racing up and down the main road. After several passes, he drove on to the parking lot of O'Donnell Pontiac and started doing donuts all over the lot. But, he couldn't resist the urge to drive by us one more time. He made his U-turn, came back and stopped. Then with a little extra gusto, he peeled wheels and took off, he and his friends laughing as they finally disappeared.

Certainly, each and every one of us had already memorized the tag number of his car, along with its color and other remarkable features. We could also describe him and his fun loving passengers, down to their positions in the car and color of the shirts they were wearing. Yet, I don't think any one in our group wanted to believe that he was that brazen or stupid.

I looked around and said, "Whoever spots that ass tomorrow, take the appropriate action."

As fate would have it, the following afternoon, I pulled off the police parking lot and he was in front of me. I turned on the overhead lights and tapped the siren to get his attention. When he pulled over, I walked up, asked for his license and registration and escorted him back to the police station.

When I told him I was going to write him a summons for his actions the previous evening, he said, "You can't write me a ticket. You were off duty and that means you don't have the authority to write me a ticket, no matter what I did."

"I'm a police officer 24 hours a day and I do indeed have the authority to write you a summons," I replied. "But, I am going to give you the biggest break and best advice you've ever had. I'm writing you one citation, and one citation only, for spinning wheels. That carries a fine of $35.00. My advice is, pay it, and that would be the smartest thing you can do."

"Bullshit. I'll see your ass in court."

I smiled. "That's up to you. But, if you come to court, I'm gonna tell the judge exactly what happened—all of it."

"I don't care. I say you can't write me a ticket, because you were off duty and you were drinkin' beer."

"Don't worry, I'll tell the judge that I was drinking beer too."

Several weeks later I went to court and, sure enough, "Hot Rod" was there. I took the stand and told Judge Robert Fisher of the District Court everything that had occurred, including the fact that I was off duty at the time, drinking beer with a group of 19 other police officers. I described, in detail, the violations that took place, confronting the defendant the following day and being told I had no authority to write him a summons.

The defense claimed that his client only broke the law after being encouraged to do so by the police officers. He said one officer, who could not be identified, had told the defendant to "get ready" and "waved him off the line."

Judge Fisher, however, didn't buy the tale of woe and found "Hot Rod" guilty. He asked if the defendant had a prior driving record and, as I was handing a copy to His Honor, the defense attorney was claiming his client had no prior record. At that point, the copy of the defendant's driving record began to unfurl like a scroll.

Judge Fisher remarked, "Oh, I bet you're proud of this."

A moment later Judge Fisher passed sentence, raising the fine from $35.00 to the maximum of $450.00, plus court costs. He added a six-month restriction to his driver's license, ordering him to drive only to and from classes and to and from work. He also informed the defendant that I was a police officer 24 hours a day and, as such, had the authority to enforce all laws of the State of Maryland.

Outside the courtroom, "Hot Rod" lamented, "God, I should've listened to you."

A Woman in Need

It was certainly one of the coldest winters I could ever remember, with winds ranging from 20 to 35 miles per hour adding to the cold. Air temperatures after dark had dipped to Zero and below for several weeks and daytime highs were barely reaching the teens. The cold was keeping crime to a minimum and, after dark, it seemed the only cars on the road were state and county police cars, or those belonging to someone who had to venture out.

The 4th Platoon was working evening shift on a Saturday and the air temperature was somewhere around a balmy five degrees. As soon as the sun dropped below the horizon and the winds increased, it looked as if we were patrolling a ghost town.

Just after 7:00 PM, the dispatcher asked me to provide a telephone number. I found a public phone that was sheltered from the wind and waited for the dispatcher's call. When I answered the phone, I was surprised to hear the voice of the wife of an officer on my squad.

"Jimmy, I've been listening to the scanner and I know you guys aren't busy. So, would you do me a really big favour?"

"What's that?"

"Send my husband home."

"Is there an emergency?"

There was a long pause before she said, "Well, no. I mean not exactly. At least not the type of emergency you normally get calls about." She paused again and I could hear her take a deep breath. "Jimmy, I know you, of all people, would understand my problem. I'm horny, and I mean, really horny, like ready to hump the bedposts horny. I wanna get laid so bad I could scream. I want a stiff dick so bad, I'm about to lose my mind."

I wasn't sure if she was saying I would understand because I was a horny s.o.b. or not, but on the other side of the coin, it was certainly a direct and very honest request. I laughed. "It's the first time I've ever had a request like this, but you can bet I'm gonna see that it's filled."

"Oh, God, thank you. Thank you."

"Should I tell your husband why I'm sending him home? I mean, should I warn him about what's in store for him?"

"Tell him. Maybe he'll come through the door with a hard-on and he can take care of my problem right there in hallway."

I laughed again. "He'll be home as soon as I can get him there."

When I hung up the phone, I called her husband and had him meet me at St. John's Plaza. When I told him about the conversation I'd just had, I don't think he believed me, not at first, anyway.

Now it was his turn to laugh. "You know, I can see my wife making a call like that, but only to you. I think she knows she can trust you with a call like that."

"Well, I'm honoring her request. Go home and take care of her problem. And, as far as questions from anyone goes, I'll just refer 'em to you. If you wanna tell everybody why you went home, that's up to you. I'm not saying a word."

There was an endless string of questions at the end of the night, but I remained true to my word. The following day when he was bombarded with questions, he said, "My wife was extremely horny and I went home to take care of her problem." Yet, I don't think anyone believed that was the reason he went home.

He spoke with me later, and asked if he should submit a leave request for the time he was off.

"Yes. But, since they don't have a 'Horny Wife Needs Satisfaction" leave category, request it as comp time. If anybody asks for a reason, I'll say you were workin' hard on an overheated furnace."

My Years with the Howard County Police Department

With Bill Seifert and A Cast of Interesting Characters

Short Fiasco

Bill, Frank Dawson and the Bar Patrons

Frank and I were dispatched to a bar fight at the Woodstock Inn and, right away, I started thinking about my new hat. Those were the days when we wore Campaign Hats, and I had a terrible time keeping mine clean, in the proper military shape and from being destroyed every time I turned around. So, here I was wearing my brand new hat to a bar fight.

When we arrived at the Woodstock Inn, some little sawed-off shit came running at me with a crab mallet. I couldn't believe this sawed-off runt was tryin' to attack me with a three-ounce, wooden crab mallet. I grabbed him and tried to put the handcuffs on him and, the next thing I knew I had slapped one of the cuffs on Frank.

Somehow, in the midst of the confusion, I got the cuff off of Frank, but that's when Frank's gun fell out of his holster. So, what did I do? I snatched it up off the ground and handed it to the nearest bystander. "Here, hold this." It didn't hit me until later that the guy could've shot us, but in the heat of the battle I wasn't thinking about that.

Meanwhile, the sawed-off shit was still tryin' to whack me with the crab mallet. I knew it was time to get serious, so I took my hat off and tossed it on to the hood of my car. That's when the undersized asshole ran up behind me and smacked me with the mallet. I grabbed the little turd and tossed him across the hood of my car. I landed on top of him and, naturally, both of us landed on my new hat, destroying it.

To add insult to the loss of my hat, back at the station I was told that, because of the size of my prisoner, I could only take credit for half an arrest.

Vacation – Take One

The Saturday morning briefing was just about over when Corporal Lilley announced, "I begin a two-week vacation at 1600 hours. Please, everyone, get me outta here on time. Most of all, that means no departmental collisions at 1530 hours."

Everybody laughed and we headed to our assigned sectors.

My day started great, when Corporal Lilley said, "Seifert, you take the unmarked car today." Well, actually he let me take the car only after I got down on my knees and begged to drive it. Then there was a death threat clause attached to my use of the car. If I damaged it, I should shoot myself or prepare for a firing squad. That would probably be a firing squad of one—Corporal Lilley emptying his revolver in my ass.

In no time at all I was driving around my assigned beat in Columbia showing off this God-awful greenish gold, Dodge. The day seemed to be going by pretty fast and it was around 1430 hours when an alarm call came in from the Merriweather Post Pavilion Office. I drove down South Entrance Road and turned off on to the access road to the office. A truck was driving out and it was a tight squeeze getting by. A little too tight, actually.

I felt the bump on the right side of the car and hit the brakes right away. It was already too late. I had committed the unthinkable sin and had a departmental collision.

I was trying to decide if I should just go ahead and shoot myself there on the access road, or call Corporal Lilley, tell him what I'd done, and have him shoot me.

His personal policy was, "Never, ever call over the radio and tell the police dispatcher that you've been involved in a departmental collision—not unless there are at least six bodies in the roadway. Just call and ask me to meet you ASAP."

His personal policy arose out of an incident a few months prior, when an officer called over the radio saying he'd been involved in a collision during a violent rainstorm. The officer had bumped a chain that was across an entrance to a business in Columbia, but there was absolutely no damage to the cruiser or the chain. By the description in the Maryland Motor Vehicle Code, there had to be damage to property, or injury to person or persons to be classified as an auto accident. But, at the end of the shift, he was ordered to write up the required paperwork, including all accompanying disciplinary action forms, because the officer had called over the radio saying he had been involved in a departmental collision. I think he completed the mandatory reports around 0400 hours. So, Corporal Lilley said that from now on he'd decide whether or not there was an accident that required a ton and half of paperwork.

I called him and asked if he could meet me ASAP, and then I just waited for him to arrive and shoot me. He pulled up beside me and I said, "God, I hate to tell you this, but I had a departmental."

A few seconds later he was looking at the right front fender of the car. He said, "Well, the molding's loose and there's one ugly ass black mark down the side of the car. But, to the eye and touch, there're no dents."

He turned and pointed a finger at me, which I thought was much better than his revolver. "Seifert, get your ass up to Penn Jersey Auto at the Golden Triangle. Pick up a can of rubbing compound, a can of wax and a tube of super glue, and meet me in the garage at the station."

Fifteen minutes later, he and I were using rubbing compound to erase that "ugly ass black mark" from the side of the car. Next, came a coat of wax and then the molding was super glued back into place.

He stepped back and smiled. "Well, that sure as hell doesn't look like a car that's been involved in a departmental." He looked at his watch. "I might get outta here on time after all."

Afterward, that can of wax and rubbing compound stayed in the trunk of Jim's car. Over the years there were a lot of stories, told over a cold beer, of how the rubbing compound and wax saved many an officer from everything to an ass chewing to loss of leave.

Vacation – Take Two

My vacation was only hours away, and the Seifert family was packed and ready to leave immediately for Disney World. Naturally, that usually meant something was going to happen to screw up our plans. But, the day was drawing to a close, and I only had to get to the station and I was gone. I was almost dancing on the seat of my cruiser when I started the drive in.

Then a giant shit hit the fan. A call was being dispatched regarding a personal injury accident that was only three blocks away. I thought about beating my head on the dash or steering wheel and screaming, but that wouldn't change things. I arrived at the accident scene and immediately got the good news from the dispatcher—the evening shift officer would handle the accident. Yes! Yes! The good news was followed quickly by bad news. I had to stay and direct traffic. Shit! Shit! Shit!

By now, black smoke was starting to rise from under the hood of one of the cars involved in the accident. I jumped out of my cruiser, ran to the trunk and grabbed the fire extinguisher. I was hurrying to the car when the first fire truck pulled up and, in no time at all, the firemen were putting out the fire.

I turned around and stomped back to my cruiser. By now, I was really pissed off because I was going to be late and delay our departure time to Disney. I was fuming by the time I threw the fire extinguisher into the trunk of the cruiser.

Ah, yes. The next, "Oh, shit. Why me?" event of the past few minutes blew up in my face.

I forgot that I had pulled the pin and activated the fire extinguisher. When it hit the floor of the trunk it went off, spraying the entire interior of the trunk and me, with that lovely yellow fire retardant. There I was lookin' like a fuckin' big yellow bird and I still had to direct traffic. Yes, and every prick that drove by, slowed down so they could get a closer look at the giant, fuzzyheaded Canary that was directing traffic.

Now, we would be even later departing for Disney, because I would hafta clean the car, replace the expended fire extinguisher and complete my reports before leaving.

God! What a great way to start a vacation.

Midnight Mystery Ride-along

I was working night shift and had called out on a foot patrol of the Oakland Mills Village Center. About a minute later, I heard Marty Gavin call Sergeant Lilley and ask him to meet him at the Wilde Lake Village Green ASAP. I laughed, thinking that Marty had one of those "don't do it" mishaps and was calling Jim to the scene. It was an extremely cold, clear night and I figured that if his screw up were bad enough, I'd be able to hear the gunfire when Jim shot him.

If you want to know Marty, I can only give you one wild ass description. Just watch The Muppet Show, or one of the Muppet Movies, and when Beaker appears, picture him in a Howard County Police Uniform and you have Marty. Well, Marty might be a little taller than Beaker.

Anyway, I finished my foot patrol and, half frozen, I jumped in my car, pulled off the lot and waited for the blast of warm air. Then I heard a strange noise and I looked around, wondering what it was and where it was coming from. I glanced in my rear-view mirror and "Holy Shit!" there was something crouched on the inside, rear window ledge.

I slammed on the brakes, jumped outta the car and that's when I saw what had to be the biggest, meanest damn cat in the world. I reached for him and he started hissing and swatting at me and I think if he could've made it to the front seat, he would've driven off with my car.

I noticed that while he was waiting for me to come back to the car, he had torn my police windbreaker to shreds. Now, the fight was on. I grabbed the hanger that once held my windbreaker and began duelling with the cat. He wasn't giving up his warm home, at least not without a nasty fight. I was on the side of the road, yelling and beating at the cat with the coat hanger, while he growled, hissed, spit and tried his best to claw my ass to ribbons. But, finally, I got him out and he sprinted across the road and disappeared down in Copperstone Circle. That's when I heard the sound of laughter. Wouldn't you know it? Some of my "best friends" were hiding and watching me fight with the cat.

True confessions came from "Beaker" Gavin later in the shift.

"I was walking foot patrol at Wilde Lake when I spotted the cat. I cornered it in the entranceway to the Slayton House and when I grabbed it, the damn thing sank his claws in my heavy winter coat. That was one pissed pussy. He wouldn't let go and I couldn't pull him off. That's when I heard you call out at Oakland Mills and I decided to call Sergeant Lilley.

"It didn't take a lotta time to persuade Jim to drive me and the cat over to your car at Oakland Mills. We were able to pry it off my coat and toss it in your car. When we slammed the door, it didn't waste any time rippin' the shit outta your police windbreaker either."

Near the end of the shift, and just about the time I was thinking I'd heard the last cat joke, I turned on my radio to listen to some music. That's when Lisa Kay, the night DJ at WCAO said, "Bill, how was your date with the pussycat?"

Singing/Dancing Recital

It was late night when I was dispatched to a burglar alarm at the backstage area of the Merriweather Post Pavilion. I arrived, along with a few other officers, and we began checking the doors for signs of a break in. It took several minutes to completely check the building and backstage area over, but we determined that it was probably just another false alarm.

I called dispatch and asked them to send a representative to check the building to make sure everything was secure. Sometimes it seems to take forever to get someone to respond to check the buildings, so there we were with boredom setting in. That's when I said I wanted to sing and dance on stage. So, naturally one of my fellow officers had to give me the "Seifert, you ain't got a hair on your ass if you don't get out there on stage and do it," challenge.

What the hell, it was just us and I proceeded to take center stage. After taking a bow to all corners I started bounding around the stage and singing. My dancing grace best compares with that of a moose, with three broken legs, trying to run from a hunter. And my singing voice—well, there's nothing quite like it. The sound is a mixture of a Screech Owl and a fire alarm.

Just as I completed my first routine of the evening, I heard the sound of someone clapping from the seats in the pavilion seat area. It seemed that the Merriweather representative had arrived early and in plenty of time to watch me make as ass of myself.

Seifert's Bits and Pieces

This is another of those, "it can only happen to me" debacles. I took my cruiser to the Columbia Car Wash and settled back for the ride through. Somewhere at about the halfway point my cruiser was rammed from behind. *What the hell was that,* I thought and looked into my rear-view mirror. There was another car right there, dead on my ass.

Well, I called my supervisor to let him know that I needed him right away at the car wash. And you guessed it, Sergeant Lilley was my supervisor. When he arrived he gave me that "You've gotta be shittin' me look" when I told him what had happened.

When he asked the other driver how he managed to hit the back of my cruiser in the car wash, the guy said, "I was trying to read what it said on the back of the car in front of. So, I drove over the rollers and ran into the back of the car."

Sergeant Lilley stared at the guy. "It says County Police. That's what's on the back of his car."

I knew Jimmy wanted to rip the guy's head off and shove it up his ass, because of all the paperwork he would hafta do, but he was very professional in the way he dealt with the situation. Then again, there were probably too many witnesses.

***

Howard County is located on the approached to BWI Airport and one morning a small plane crashed into a house at the end of a cul-de-sac in Columbia, killing all on board. The plane had hit the ground in front of the house, flipped over and went through the front of the house. The front end of the plane ended up in the basement, with the tail section pointing into the air.

One of the officers responding to the call asked the radio operator for the exact address of the incident. Before the dispatcher could answer, Sergeant Lilley, who was already on the scene, said, "Don't worry, you can't miss it. It's the only house with a plane sticking out of it."

***

There was a remote control model airplane park near Columbia, and I used to stop by now and then to watch the show. The planes varied in size and a few people even had remote controlled helicopters. One day as I was passing by the park, one of the "pilots" lost control of their helicopter and it started spinning and diving. And, yes, you bet your pay check it fell out of the sky and into my cruiser.

I thought I'd make a joke of it and called over the police radio that a helicopter had just crashed into my police car. That's when I found out how many people have police scanners.

It seems that police headquarters was swamped with calls from concerned citizens and every news agency, and other media source out there. And, because others couldn't take a joke, I was on the receiving end of a giant ass chewing.

***

Late on a winter evening, the county was hit by a nasty ice

storm, which caused accidents by the dozen. It wasn't long before I was dispatched to a multi-car accident on one of the rural roads. The dispatcher couldn't pinpoint the exact location of the accident and I headed in the general direction, hoping for an update as to where it was.

I popped over the crest of a hill and there, right in front of me, were six or seven cars on and off the road. Some were in the middle of the road and others were in the ditch. As I took my foot off the gas, I hit a patch of ice and started spinning. What a wild ass ride that was. I'm spinning in circles, passing by the cars and the people standing on the roadway, and the people were staring at me as I went whirling on by them, and slid backward into a ditch.

Soon, everybody was running over to check on me and when I said I was there to help them, they burst into fits of laughter. When the laughter toned down, we worked together to push all of the cars back on to the road and send everyone on their way.

They thanked me very much for my help, but not one of them complimented me on my driving skills.

Lakefront Riot

Bruce Harrison, a long time friend and K-9 Officer, and I were dispatched to the lakefront in Columbia for a reported fight. It was a hot and muggy evening, and there was a very large crowd gathered at the lakefront because of a free concert. And, surely there was plenty of booze flowing and drugs being used. You can guess the mood of the crowd.

We approached a group, where some guy was trying to fight with anybody and everybody. He was so screwed up he didn't know where he was or what he was doing. Bruce tried to arrest the guy, but he turned around and punched Bruno, Bruce's dog, right in the head. That's when Bruce kicked the guy in the balls so hard, he lifted him off the ground, but the asshole just grinned at us and took off running toward a bigger group.

Bruce ran after the guy and I was right behind him. Before we knew it, the crowd surrounded us, and we were getting punched, kicked and hit with coolers, bottles and anything else these assholes could get their hands on. Bruce had Bruno on a long lead and he was trying to keep the crowd back with the dog. But when the dog lunged at them from one direction, they would turn and come at us from another. Now, the heat was beginning to take its toll on us, and we were just about drained.

Both of us called a Signal 13 (Officer Needs Help) over our radios, and in this case we were in dire need of help. Well, some damn supervisor, who was sitting on his fat ass in the police station, cancelled the 13s. You'd think when two officers call back-to-back Signal 13s, one of them being a K-9 Officer, he'd send help without question. Thank God, nobody obeyed his order.

I got as close to Bruce as I could and we tried to battle our way out of the crowd. All of a sudden, I felt a sharp pain in my right thigh. Obviously I had gotten too close to Bruce and, in the heat of battle, Bruno didn't recognize friend from foe, and sank his teeth into me.

"Bruce, your fuckin' dog just bit me," I yelled.

"The son-of-a-bitch bit me, too," he yelled back.

Well, so much for sympathy. Now, back to the fight to get our asses outta there alive.

Finally, the troops started arriving from everywhere— Howard County Police, Maryland State Police, Baltimore County Police, Anne Arundel County Police and I think Prince George's County sent officers as well.

Bruce and I made it up over the hill and away from the crowd. That's when I saw Corporal Jim Lilley getting out of his car. I know he was off duty and called from home, and I loved the attire he arrived in. He was dressed in blue jeans, running shoes, police uniform shirt, gun belt, riot helmet and carrying a riot baton. I knew things were about to change.

Captain Robey and Colonel Rappaport (Chief of Police) called Jim over and told him he was now in charge of clearing the entire lakefront. I recall someone saying that a bottle, which was thrown as soon as he got out of his car, had hit Colonel Rappaport.

When we started to gather for instructions, Beaker was there along with Bruce, and I remember Harry Monroe, Larry Freer, Barry

Boone and Sam Hammond and K-9 Officers from several area police departments.

Jim's orders were very clear. "It's open season on these cocksuckers. Anybody that assaults a police officer goes to the hospital. If you tell an asshole to move and they don't—hit 'em. If they don't move fast enough—hit 'em. The lakefront's now closed. Gentlemen, let's go."

And, closed it was. That night marked the last of the free concerts, and it was also the incident that caused alcoholic beverages to be banned from all lakefront activities. Then came the County Ordinance barring open containers of alcoholic beverages at all times.

Pet Pagan

The Pagans Motorcycle Gang had a clubhouse located just off of U. S. Route One, but we rarely had any type of daily contact with them. Late one evening there was a fight call dispatched at a bar off of Meadowridge Road and, when we arrived, there was a large group of Pagans on the parking lot. But, the fight was over.

One of the Pagans looked exactly Donald Sutherland's character in the movie The Dirty Dozen. Except this guy was at least 6'8" tall, with the IQ of an oyster and he was much crazier than Donald Sutherland's character. To say the least, he was scary.

Naturally, there was some limp dick wimp on the parking lot too, and he was still guzzling beer. As usual, with assholes like him, his balls started getting bigger with each sip of beer and the arrival of more police officers. Pretty soon, he was flexing his beer balls, yelling at the Pagans, and telling us what we should be doing. While doing his beer balls strut, he got too close to the Pagans and a fist flew out of the crowd, knocking the little weasel on his ass. At the time, I was standing beside the Pagan who hit him and "Donald Sutherland" was standing on my left.

Now, with his balls deflated, he's on his feet, screaming and yelling, "Did you see that? Did you see that? Arrest him. Arrest him."

Hey, I wanted to punch the little limp dick myself, so I said,

"Sorry, buddy, I didn't see a thing."

All of a sudden, "Donald Sutherland" is my new best friend. He grabbed me and gave me a bear hug, and started following me around the parking lot like a puppy dog. He's laughing and telling his friends that I'm a really funny guy, and I can't get rid of him.

After about 15 minutes of him following me around, I turned to another officer. "You know what's gonna be great? If this guy follows me home, I'm gonna ask my wife if I can keep him."

I don't know what it was about my comment, but it upset him and he started to get pissed off. Other members of the Pagans ended up grabbing him and taking him away. I was kinda upset. I really thought I was gonna have my very own Pet Pagan.

When the Ghouls Come Out

I never understood the fascination some people seem to have when there's a fatal accident, bloody crime scene, or other mishaps where there is an abundance of gore and torn flesh. Yet, they always come out of their caves or lairs, or wherever they come from when police officers and rescue personnel are trying to investigate the crime, or render aid to the injured. Some have arrived with cameras in hand and, I often wondered if they kept scrapbooks in their homes labelled "Blood and Guts" or "Carnage" to entertain guests at parties. Some of the ghouls have gotten belligerent when told to stay back from a car, or even a body lying in the roadway. Every now and then, one of the "living dead" ends up being arrested for interfering with, or hindering the investigation.

On a night shift, I arrived on the scene of a fatal accident where a car had crashed and burned, and the driver was still in the vehicle. Out of nowhere a crowd started to assemble and before long it was rather large. As usual, they were pushing forward, trying to get a look at the corpse and generally being a pain in our asses.

On this particular night, I had brought a steak sandwich for lunch. So, being the warped pervert that I am, I went to my cruiser and broke off an ample piece of the rare steak. I walked over to the car, made a production of checking things out and, before turning around, reached inside the car. A few seconds later I stood up, turned and began eating the steak. When I got near the crowd I called out to the police and firemen, "You know, once you get through the crust, the meat's pretty tender."

Some of the curious wannabe vampires started to choke and gag, but suddenly most of the crowd left. The police and firemen laughed so hard, a few almost pissed themselves.

Flashlight Dilemma

It was said that a person could tell how long a cop had been on the job by the size of the flashlight he carried. As a rookie, most of us carried a five or six cell flashlight but, by the time I retired, I carried a Double AA light on my gun belt.

When I was a young officer, I responded to a report of a breaking and entering that had just occurred. It was snowing, but the ground was still very soft and wet. When I arrived, I went to the back of the house to see if a suspect might still be in the vicinity.

After checking and finding nothing, I stuck my six cell light in the loop and began to walk toward the front of the house. About two or three steps up a slight incline, I slipped and fell. Naturally, my graceful dive brought a round of applause and laughter from my back up officers. My light lodged in the soft ground and I landed in such a way that the light jammed up under my ribs. The pain was intense and I lagged behind my "friends" cursing and swearing for a minute.

When I got myself together, I went into the house to talk with the victim, but every few minutes I had to leave the room and catch my breath. The victim kept giving me a strange look, while the other officers laughed. I managed to process the scene and complete my report, but not without difficulty.

As soon as I cleared the call, I went straight to the hospital, where I found that I had several cracked ribs and a bruise that ran from my left armpit to my hip. I just shook my head, because I knew this was going to be joke material for the next few days, maybe even weeks.

Victim of the Mud Monster

Back in the mid 70s, my squad leader, Corporal Jim Lilley, was building a log home in western Howard County. As I happened to be working that particular beat, I decided to stop by to check on the progress of the house. As with any construction site, it was very muddy and, yes, yours truly discovered that police cars couldn't drive on top of the mud.

In no time at all, the infamous "Mud Monster" had my car in its clutches, and I was sinking fast. I figured that, with my luck, the mud would soon be up over the hood and oozing through all the windows.

I knew that I was in a lot more than deep mud. The High Command, at that time, took even the slightest scratch or misuse, which surely included getting stuck in this mushy brown mire, as a personal attack on them. To make matters worse, if there was such a thing, Sergeant Roger Neubauer was sitting in his squad car on West Watersville Road, watching my car sink. I was sure he'd beat a path to headquarters to report my "mishap" and help erect the gallows for my hanging when I returned to the station.

Calling a tow truck would require giving a reason for the request and would alert the High Command that they'd soon be hosting a castration party. As usual, Jim had an idea for saving my testicles and/or neck. He called one of the men over who had been working on the house, but was now laughing at my sinking problem. The next thing I knew this guy, who was really big and looked strong enough to pick up my car and drag it outta the mud, was climbing on to a bulldozer. A few seconds later the bulldozer was headed straight for my car.

Holy shit! Jim's gonna have this guy bury me right here, I thought.

Well, it turned out that this gentleman, with the dark beard, was a magician with the dozer. Somehow, he was able to gently lift and nudge my car out of the mud without leaving a scratch. For a second or two I thought about running over and kissing the guy, but I figured I wasn't his type. Besides, I didn't really wanna kiss a guy with a beard.

When I looked back, Sergeant Neubauer was gone and I feared the worst. I went to the car wash and, after about 30 minutes work, it was clean and about a ton lighter. I drove to the station, expecting to be on the carpet immediately, but nobody said a word.

A few minutes later, Roger walked by, nodded and grinned. I didn't know if he was grinning because of me getting stuck, or the puddle of sweat around my chair.

Body Armor for Two

In the early days of "bulletproof" vests, the department did not issue them, so we had to buy our own. Of course, I bought one, and immediately put a Superman emblem on the front of it. Initially, it was tough (at least for me) to get used to wearing the vest and, it was also very hot during the summer months. Instead of being worn, mine ended up staying the in the car most of the time.

Tommy Watkins and I were dispatched to a man with a gun call and arrived at the same time. I got out of my car with the vest and handed it to Tommy and told him to wear it. He promptly shoved it back in my hands and said, "No, you wear it."

I pushed it back at him. "No, you wear it."

"You wear it, Seifert."

"Bullshit, Watkins. You wear it."

For over a minute we stood on the sidewalk, pushing and shoving the vest back and forth between us. Our "discussion" over who was or was not going to wear the vest got rather heated and we were yelling at each other. Finally, neither of us put it on.

We walked up and knocked on the door of the apartment and a man, with a very confused look on his face, answered. When we asked him about the gun, he said he looked out the window when we arrived and saw us arguing, and was sure that we were gonna start fighting or possibly shoot each other. At that point, he was certain the department had sent two insane police officers to his apartment so, for his own safety, he locked the gun in a closet.

Family Affair

One of the first times I was hit with a punch was by accident. I was investigating an accident in Elkridge, where a car had rolled down a hill. The driver was a local male, accompanied by a female companion. The guy was very nervous and was unwilling to give me the female's name. Of course, it wasn't unusual for many men traveling along the Route One corridor to have strange women with them. Almost the entire strip was noted for easy access motels, which made it a "paradise" for men bringing hookers out from the city.

After a few minutes the guy told me he was married and didn't want his wife to find out he was out with another woman. But, he seemed just a little too nervous to suit me and I continued questioning him about the girl. Finally, he gave in and told me the girl's name. It turned out she was his sister. At that point, she burst into tears and I had to calm her down before continuing with my investigation.

Sometime during all of this, the area supervisor arrived and I told him the guy was with his sister. He shrugged his shoulders and walked away.

While I was climbing back up the hill, I heard the supervisor say to the guy, "So, I hear you're fuckin' your sister."

The guy instantly goes crazy, starts screaming and takes a swing at the supervisor. Well, naturally, the supervisor ducked and I walked right into the punch. My balance, walking up the hill, wasn't the greatest and the next thing I knew I was rolling ass overhead back down the embankment.

I scrambled back up to the top of the hill, and slammed the guy to the ground after telling him he was under arrest for assaulting a police officer. The whole time I was handcuffing him he was yelling, "I didn't mean to hit you. I was trying to hit that other mutha fucker."

As years passed, I found that a situation could go from great, right to hell when somebody else made a smart-ass comment.

A Life Changing Moment

While investigating an accident, a drunk pulled a switchblade and tried to attack me. He was so drunk he could barely stand, let alone play "carve the policeman" with a knife. But, he really pissed me off and I grabbed the asshole by the throat with one hand, and grabbed a handful of hair with the other. Then I "pushed" his face into the hood of the car several times.

At the same time, my wife, Lou, and daughter, Amanda, were driving by. So, I stopped pounding the asshole and waved before going back to adjusting the attitude of the drunk. Later that night, my wife told me she said to Amada, "Oh, look, there's Daddy working." Just as quickly she said, "No. Don't watch." I guess she didn't want Amanda to see Daddy smacking the shit outta "blade man."

Years later, I was just about to walk into a restaurant for lunch, when I heard a man yelling my name. I looked around and saw a guy running across five lanes of traffic and continuing to call my name. As he got closer I realized it was the guy who had pulled the switchblade on me and I thought he wanted a rematch.

The next thing I knew he was thanking me and shaking my hand. He said when I arrested him it changed his life. After his arrest, he voluntarily entered treatment for his drinking problem, went back to school, got married and landed a good job. And, he said he owed it all to me.

That was one of only a few times that a person I'd arrested thanked me for smashing his face into the hood of a car. Maybe in the joy of seeing me again he forgot that part.

Hot Landing Zone

Shortly before I retired, I was working a midnight shift on Route One and it had been one of those boring nights. I was really tired when I headed back to the station, which sure as hell meant that something would happen on the way in. And, in the blind of an eye, the dispatcher was broadcasting a call for a very serious accident on Route 29 near Route 40 in Ellicott City. At the same time, the MSP Medivac helicopter was being dispatched to the scene and told to land in the southbound lanes of Route 29.

The officers on the accident scene were told to switch over to another channel, while I remained on the primary channel. So, I was headed northbound on Route 29 and nearing the location of the collision. Soon, I noticed officers waving and yelling and, being tired, I naturally assumed they were happy to see me and were waving a friendly "Hi, Billy."

I smiled and waved back just as I passed another group that was waving and yelling. At the same instant I saw the helicopter directly in front of me. Holy shit! I was looking directly at the pilot and he was looking right back at me and, I'm sure, we both showed the same facial expression—scared shitless. I turned sharply to the right as he pulled up.

I found out that the instructions to the pilot had been changed and he was instructed to land in the northbound lanes instead of the southbound lanes. But, I didn't hear those orders because I was still on the primary channel. Well, that meant that my friends were not waving a cheerful "Hi, Billy" as I was going by. They were waving and yelling, "You dumb shit, you're about to drive into the fuckin' helicopter."

With some of the stupid shit many of us did over the years, I sometimes wonder how we managed to survive until retirement.

Trying to get Home

It had been a very long evening shift. You know the kind I'm talkin' about—the one that just doesn't wanna end. When it finally came to a close, I only wanted to have a coffee, go home and collapse.

I stopped by the Dunkin' Donuts on Route 40 with another officer and had just sat down at the counter, when someone started pounding on the window. I looked over my shoulder and knew this had to be some asshole that wanted to screw with us because we were cops in uniform. That, and the fact that he was probably drunk and had nothing better to do.

I turned my back on him, took a sip of my coffee and hoped he would go away or go climb in the Dumpster, or fall off the curb—anything, but leave me alone. But, he wouldn't take the hint and wouldn't leave, even after I yelled that we were off duty. I tried telling him to go to a phone and call the station, but the dumb dick wouldn't listen.

I tried to ignore the guy and drink my coffee, so he finally gave up pounding on the window and came inside. He said he was sorry for being such a pest, but wanted to get some advice from us regarding a problem he had. He figured since we were police officers we would be able to help him. Now, he says that his girlfriend had stabbed him and he wasn't sure what to do. At first, I thought he was joking, but he turned around and showed us the stab wounds.

I damn near fell off the counter stool, but kept my composure and called the station to request an ambulance and on duty officer. That's when the night suddenly got longer—much, much longer. Somehow, the other officer and me got hosed into taking the report, doing the paperwork and arresting the guy's girlfriend.

The sun was coming up when I finally left to go home.

Beat Me, Whip Me and I'll Pay You

Yes, it was another midnight shift and time for my nightly eye opener. I stopped by the 7-11 on Route 40 to grab a coffee and get my nightly caffeine fix. While I was pouring my coffee, a young man came into the store and walked over to me. He was very polite and asked if he could talk to me and offered to buy my coffee.

As I was walking out the front door with the young man, Officer Don Bathgate was getting out of his car. So, the kid said he wanted to buy Don's coffee as well.

While Donnie was in the store, I asked the young man what he wanted to talk to me about. All of a sudden, he got this weird look on his face as if he was expecting his head to start spinning around. Then, he started screaming that he wanted me to beat him with my nightstick. Naturally, there was a crowd on the lot and everybody is staring at us while this kid keeps screaming at me to beat him. He reached into his pocket, pulled out a wad of money and starts throwing it at me. While throwing the money at me, he's screaming, "beat me, kill me." Then he jumped on me and kept screaming, "Please, beat me. Kill me."

About that time, Donnie walked out of the 7-11 and saw the kid attacking me. Well, Don Bathgate was truly one of the strongest people I've ever met, and with a little help from him, I got the cuffs on the guy and we hauled him to the station. There, it didn't take long to find out this guy was an escapee from a state hospital.

Soon, he was very calm and talking to me again like we had been friends forever. Then he started crying and sobbing over his lack of a love life.

That's when Donnie asked him if he had a problem with girls, and the guy goes nuts again.

He began screaming, jumped over the table and attacked Donnie. I tried not to laugh, but the kid looked like some cartoon character. Donnie was holding him in one hand, the kid's feet dangling in the air, with his arms spinning like a windmill. He just held him like that until he calmed down and everything returned to normal. But, when you're a cop, what is normal on the midnight shift, or any shift for that matter?

Code Blue

I was dispatched to the Emergency Room at Howard County General Hospital for a report of a guy on drugs that was becoming violent. With as much time as I seemed to spend at the ER, I knew most of the staff working that night. When I arrived, the nurses didn't say anything when I started into the room, they just laughed. That should've been a hint to wait for another officer, but I went in anyway.

Two steps into the room, I stopped dead in my tracks and burst out laughing. The guy, who I found out later was on LSD, was sitting on the bed, half-naked and painted blue. I guess my laughing must've pissed the guy off, because he went berserk and attacked me. In no time at all, we were rolling around the room, breaking up every item of furniture in there, including the bed.

The nurses charged in and tried to give the guy a shot, but they couldn't get close to him. They left, and I continued my battle with the oversized Smurf, hoping somebody would hurry the hell up and get there to help me with this idiot.

Finally, Howard Cogle, who I always described as 7 feet 13 inches tall and 260 pounds of very solid flesh arrived. After Howard gave one of his notorious "Ha, Ha, Ha, Ha," laughs, he grabbed the Tripping Blue Smurf and pulled him off me. He was easily able to hold the guy in the air until the nurses harpooned him in the ass, or some place with a shot and knock him out.

I told the nurses it would've been nice if they warned me before I went in the room, but they thought it would be funny to let me go in without the warning. I know I got a big "ho fuckin' ho" out of it.

Triple Nut Sundae

I don't know why, but it always seemed that I got the calls where someone was on the verge of losing their sanity, looking for their sanity, or had already gone around the bend and completely lost it. I often wondered if someone in the department thought I could relate to them, because they thought my sanity was, at times very questionable, or they thought it was entertaining to send me to these calls. Then again, maybe I looked like I should be called "Doctor Seifert, friend to the Nut Sundaes."

Anyway, here I was responding to a call for a female throwing items from a third story window. When I arrived at the address, I noticed potted plants strewn all over the ground and the headlights had been broken out of all the parked cars. I hurried up the stairs and into the apartment, which was filled with smoke.

The woman said she wanted to bake a box of old letters and photographs and had put them in the oven. I told her I was certain that the letters and pictures were done and she could turn off the oven. Then I worried that she might ask me to help her eat them, so I quickly moved to the next topic—potted plants and headlights.

She said plants need lots of air, so she tossed them out the window. As for the headlights, they were staring at her. The only way she could get them to stop staring at her was to break them.

God, why me? I thought, while looking around the apartment. That's when I noticed that the walls were covered with dozens of old photographs of her with the Kennedys, various congressmen and senators, high-ranking government officials and Hollywood stars. There were also diplomas from several very well know universities, documenting the degrees she held.

I convinced her that it was time to go visit the nice man at the hospital, where she could sit in a quiet padded room. On the way there, I stopped at a traffic light and a car, occupied by several young, Black Males, pulled up beside me. The back window was partially opened, and she yelled to them. "Hey, I had oral sex with Sammy Davis, Jr."

They laughed and shook their heads, probably thinking, "better you than me."

***

Naturally, I was dispatched to the call for a man running around in a bar, wearing a garter belt, fishnet stockings and spiked high heels. He was trotting around the bar, throwing shit at the patrons, while yelling strange sayings and uttering weird chants.

After I took him into custody, I found out that he had been to the bar a number of times. On those occasions he was wearing a bra and sat alone drinking, but not bothering the other patrons. So, they let him drink and didn't bother to call.

I gave him a ride to the hospital, so he could talk to the doctor and maybe explain the reason for his attire. While at the hospital, I found that the guy was vice president of a well-known university. Wow! A well educated cross dresser.

***

A doctor, actually a psychiatrist, lived in a house on Mink Hollow Road near the Howard County/Montgomery County line. He had a good reputation and was very well known throughout the community. He would sometimes call in, reporting suspicious persons or speeding cars on Mink Hollow Road, so he was also fairly well known by many of our officers. And, I had had a few contacts with him early on in my career.

A call was dispatched, reporting that a man was obstructing traffic on the bridge, which connected Howard and Montgomery Counties. When the officer arrived on the scene, he found a man had put up a table and chair, and was stopping cars that were trying to cross into Howard County from Montgomery County. He was asking for identification to prove place of residence and, anyone not residing in Howard County was being told they had to pay a toll to enter. After a few minutes, the officer identified the man as the very well known psychiatrist. Now, was the good doctor trying to have a little fun at the motorists' expense, or had he spent too much time dealing with those of questionable sanity and gone over to the other side?

After some coaxing, the tollbooth was closed and all was

peaceful. But it soon started again. I'm not sure how many calls were received about the doctor trying to collect fees from non-residents of Howard County, but it took some time to convince him that he had no right to operate a tollbooth.

It was quiet for weeks, maybe even a few months before the next call came in. This time, the caller told the dispatcher that a man was trying to cut up the wooden bridge with a chainsaw. And, sure enough, there he was attacking the structure with a chainsaw.

His reasoning—if he couldn't collect a toll from all the non-residents, then he was going to prevent them from entering Howard County via Mink Hollow Road. Of course, he couldn't understand why he didn't have the right to destroy the bridge.

Well, it was definitely time for the doctor to see a doctor and possibly spend a few days or weeks in the funny room.

I don't think any of us ever really understood what happened to him. However, after a few more bizarre incidents at his home and near the county line, we received a call reporting that he had taken his own life.

More Life and Times with the Howard County Police

With Tommy Watkins and Marty "Beaker" Gavin

Midnight Heat

The nothing is sacred rule was always in play and wives and girlfriends were often the focal point. The nightly games most often involved one officer calling over the radio that he was out of service, but very busy at another officer's house. Sometimes this brought a quick volley of responses. "I'm next. Reserve a time for me. Is she working all night?"

It was no different on the Third Platoon and one particular night the game began prior to the night shift briefing. Gavin fired the first volley, zeroing in on Jim Dawson.

"Hey, J. D., don't worry while you're out west tonight. Tommy and I can drop by and keep Sue company."

"Maybe I should call ahead and make an appointment," Watkins said. "You know how long the line gets at their house."

J. D. laughed and shrugged off the comments, knowing that anything he said would only add fuel to the fire.

Not long after the 0300 time check was given, Tommy (314) called Beaker (323). "I was just at the address on Sebring Drive and I was number 923 in line."

Gavin replied, "I don't wanna wait in a line that long. Can you get me a number while you're there and call me when it's close to my turn?"

"I'll take care of it."

J. D. decided it was time to get into the act. "Okay, boys, just don't forget to leave your money on the nightstand."

Watkins never missed a beat. "314 to 323, do you have change for a nickel?"

Traffic Stop

Mike said, "I was driving west on Route 40 and, I guess, it was just after midnight when I noticed the police car behind me. I didn't pay much attention to it, because I was driving the speed limit, maybe even a little below. After I went through the traffic light at St. John's Lane and Route 40, I heard the siren, looked in the rear-view mirror and saw the red and blue flashing lights. I knew the light was green when I went through it and I wasn't speeding, so I couldn't understand why I was being pulled over.

I pulled over on to the right shoulder and stopped. I glanced in the side mirror and the rear-view mirror, but didn't see the officer get out of his car. Then all of a sudden, I heard this voice snapping commands over a PA system.

"Driver of the yellow Ford, listen very, very carefully to my instructions."

What the hell's goin' on, I thought.

"Put both hands outside the window."

I hesitated for a second or two.

"Put your hands outside the window, or I'll open fire."

Open fire! Open fire! I stuck my hands out the window so fast and so far I almost broke my ribs. Not to mention that I damn near shit myself right then and there. *What the hell was goin' on?*

"Driver, using the outside handle, very slowly open the car door."

I moved my hand as slow as possible toward the door handle, wondering when I'd either faint, shit, puke or piss all over myself. I finally pulled the handle and pushed the door open as far as I could without falling out.

"Diver, step outta the car very slowly. Keep your hands in sight and don't make any sudden moves. Any sudden moves and I'll shoot."

Christ, he was threatening to shoot me again. But, I worked my way outta the car like I was told and was very surprised that my bowels and bladder were still holding on.

"Now, with your left hand, close the car door."

I closed the door and waited. A few seconds later, the next commands came.

"Lean forward and put your hands on the roof of your car. That's good. Now, ease your legs back as far as possible and spread 'em. That's it. Spread your legs a little more. That's good."

I don't mind telling you, I was shaking so hard I thought I'd tip the car over. I didn't know what I'd done, but I was sure it was a case of mistake identity. But, I wasn't in a position to argue and I was sure the cop would shoot me if I moved. I was wondering what would happen next, when the voice called over the PA again.

"Listen carefully."

What the hell did he think I was gonna do?

"I want you to follow my next command to the letter. If you understand, nod your head twice."

I nodded twice, and realized how much I was sweating. My heart was still in my throat and I prayed I wouldn't have a heart attack and die there on the side of Route 40.

"Take off all your clothes and skip down the street naked. This is a hold up."

Take off my clothes! Skip down the street naked! It's a hold up! What the fuck's goin' on?

The police car pulled up just behind mine and the interior light went on. Inside, I saw that crazy ass Tommy Watkins laughin' his ass off. He waved, gave me the finger and sped away.

The Car Chase

Tommy Watkins was working night shift when he saw a car driving at a snail's pace on Little Patuxent Parkway in Columbia. A quick glance across the median and he said he wasn't certain that anyone was behind the wheel.

He turned around and very quickly caught up with the car. He turned on the overhead lights and gave a quick turn of the siren, but the car continued on at a "blazing" 15 miles per hour.

The code for a high speed chase is 10-80, but Tommy keyed the mic and said, "Headquarters, I have a 10-40 on LPP, that's half a 10-80. This guy's driving way too slow to call this a high speed chase."

With the help of Marty Gavin and few others he was able to get the car stopped. The driver turned out to be a 14-year old who had never driven before. He said he took his mother's car out just to see what it was like.

Felony Shoes

It seemed the night shift always provided a way for Watkins and Gavin to get into something strange. So, when they called out on a routine check at Howard County General Hospital, everything held true to form.

Marty said, "We were walking toward the entrance when I saw this crazy looking animal of some sort on the south side of the building. We started walking toward it and it turned to run away. Tommy and I took off running and actually caught up to it. We corralled it in a corner and started laughing.

"We had no idea what the hell it was, but it had long floppy ears and pretty large feet, especially the back feet. We were able to pick it up, so we carried it back to our cars.

"Tommy went inside the hospital and managed to scrounge a large cardboard box. Then we put the thing in the box and on the backseat of Tommy's car.

"Of course, we had to call our sergeant to meet us and we used the old ASAP trick to get him there as quick as possible.

"As soon as he pulled up he saw us laughing and knew it was either a good joke or we'd fucked up and needed help."

"Okay, what the hell did you do this time?" he said when he got out of his car.

We both said, "Sarge, can you tell us what this is?"

Tommy opened the back door of his cruiser and pointed to the box. About that time this head pops up through the top and I swear the long ears wiggled.

Well, the good sergeant starts laughing and says, "Holy shit! It looks like a giant rabbit."

That's what we thought too, but none of us had ever seen a rabbit that big. After a laugh filled discussion we decided that it had to belong to somebody who lived near the hospital and they'd call when they discovered it was missing.

For the rest of the night it rode with Tommy, responding to calls with him and stopping for coffee and a snack at the 7-11. His "ride-along" proved to be a big hit wherever he went and the clerk at the 7-11 even offered him a peanut butter cracker, which he ate. Soon he had a sip of coffee, a soda, a little water and ate a piece of a chocolate cupcake and God knows what else during the night.

When Tommy carried him into the station in the morning at the end of our shit, he proved to be the highlight of the hit parade.

Somebody noticed the size of the rabbit's feet and laughed. "Now those things are real felony shoes."

The term "felony shoes" came about when a thug fled from two officers who staked out a local business. The business had been victimized a number of times and they wanted desperately to catch the party responsible. Well, he broke in and when they tried to arrest him he took off and left them in the dust. Not long afterward it was said that he'd escaped so easily because he was wearing the new and improved "felony shoes." And, that term just wouldn't go away.

Soon, everybody was taking pictures of Tommy holding the rabbit and showing off his feet, or "felony shoes." Next, he was paraded around the station and had more pictures taken.

Sometime after 0800 an officer peeked out of the briefing room door and said, "Hey, Sarge, I think the owner of that rabbit you guys have is on the phone."

He took the phone and the room fell silent as we listened to his side of the conversation.

"Yes, ma'am, we have your rabbit.

"So, you think he pushed the door in the sunroom open and escaped. Oh, you forgot to lock it.

"French rabbit. You paid over $2,000 for him. Wow!

"And he has a strict diet. Eats only specially prepared food.

"Was he well taken care of? Ma'am, I assure you he was given the utmost care by the officers who found him.

"Yes, ma'am, you can drive to the police station and pick him up. Yes, ma'am, he'll be at the front desk with the Duty Officer. No. No, ma'am, no reward is necessary and we certainly couldn't accept anything for catching and caring for him."

When he hung up the phone, everybody started laughing. A second later Tommy said, "Well, tonight when she walks into the sunroom, she'll find how much he's changed after spending a night with us. He'll be lying back on a lounge chair, drinking a cold beer, smoking a cigarette and reading Hustler."

Confessions of the Author

Yours truly and friends

This work would not be a complete truth if I didn't step up to confess some of my "sins" of perverted humor. And might I begin by saying "Bless me, Father, for I am guilty of many humorous deeds." However, some would say isn't time to confess all of them.

In the early days of my career, Jim Robey (Now Maryland State Senator Jim Robey) and I were partners in the Howard County Police Department's first drug unit. On a Saturday evening in late fall, we were scouring the streets of Columbia looking for a car that was supposed to be occupied by some of our local drug "friends." Jim had received information, from a very good source, that they would be picking up drugs to take to a party for distribution.

After about a 45-minute search we spotted the car and began to follow from a reasonable distance. It didn't take long to guess that these guys were absolutely paranoid.

They made left turns, right turns, U-turns and, surely, a dozen pre-planned stops over the next hour and a half.

During this time, Jim had been sipping a Coke and suddenly Mother Nature was beckoning. But, he feared that making a stop to answer her call would result in our failing to nail these guys with the drugs. So, he decided he'd wait and, naturally, with each passing minute Mother's call was growing more urgent. Indeed, all of us have had this problem on more than one occasion and can relate to Jim's predicament.

I had just made a turn from South Entrance Road on to Old Columbia Road, when Jim practically yelled, "That's it, I can't wait another minute. Pull over, I've gotta piss."

Well, there wasn't exactly a lot of shoulder room on Old Columbia Road. In fact, on the passenger's side of the car there was an embankment and, the angle of the slope, at the place where I stopped made it almost impossible to scale. And, of course, there were no trees to hide behind.

I braked to a quick stop, turned off the lights and Jim bailed out of the car. To this day, I'll never know why he darted to the front of the car. But, there he was, standing directly in line with the headlights and, yes temptation was rearing its head and saying, "go ahead, do it."

As all of us who have had the problem of holding it for what seems like forever also know that when the damn breaks, and that almost breathless, wonderful relief is fast upon us, the water flow isn't stopped on a whim.

Out of nowhere, the hand of the devil himself reached over and turned on the high beam headlights, the four way flashers, the red grill lights and siren.

Back in those days, Jim, at 5' 10", was tipping the scales at around 225 pounds, but in no time at all, he was a nimble, dancing, screaming maniac. He was yelling something, while pissing all over the road, the hood of the car, his foot and probably his hand, about turning off the lights and siren, but I was truly fascinated by his dancing skills. I say, in all honesty, I have never seen such moves on the dance floor anywhere before, or since that night.

I believe that, on a chilly, fall, Saturday evening, Jim Robey performed the Twist, the Bird, the Limbo and invented a version of the Electric Slide, the Hustle, a rendition of Line Dancing, and many unheard of dances. And, talk about dexterity—he accomplished these amazing feats with his pecker in his hand.

The Physical Fitness Test

It was back in the early 70s, fitness was the big craze and it seemed like a good time to screw with the masses. And, what better way to screw with your fellow workers, than to mention fitness and pay raise in the same memo.

One of my closest friends, Herman Charity, was a fitness buff and he and I had been working out forever it seemed. I talked to Herman about having a little fun with the troops and he liked the idea. So, I sat down and composed a memo from the Chief of Police to all Personnel.

The body of the letter stated clearly that all police personnel would henceforth be required to pass a semi-annual physical fitness test. Those failing the test, would have their yearly pay raise held back until such time as they were able to achieve the minimum requirements set forth in the newly instituted Departmental Fitness Standards.

All personnel were to contact either Corporal James Lilley or Corporal Herman Charity to arrange the time to take their initial fitness test. The goal of the primary test would be to determine the officer's level of fitness and, afterward, a diet and exercise program would be recommended by the instructors for them to follow. The test would consist of push-ups, sit-ups and a timed one-mile run.

A copy was placed in the Patrol Notices and read out at the morning, evening and night shift briefings. There was an immediate, collective scream heard throughout the department, with cries of lawsuit and other threats flying about like paper airplanes.

Of course, those whose fitness level left much to be desired, screamed loudest and longest. Yet, a few of those who were out of out of shape approached Herman and I, asking for a date, time and location to take their test. They were ready and willing to have their fitness level determined, and prepared to follow a diet and exercise program that would be beneficial to them. And, none of them said a word about their annual pay raise as their incentive.

It took almost a week to convince everyone that the "order" was only a practical joke.

Uniform Wear Regulations

Over a period of years, many of the Howard County Police Department's rules and regulations were revised and updated, or replaced. Uniform wear regulations always seemed to be a popular topic, and many officers argued that those who wrote the orders were not required to wear the same uniform and equipment as those men and women assigned to patrol.

Certainly this presented an ideal subject for a "new" Uniform Wear Regulation. So, I sat down and penned a regulation that was sure to open the doors of exasperation.

When it was completed, I knew the perfect man to read out the new order at the dayshift briefing was Lieutenant Howard Cogle. He chuckled while reading through it and said he thought it would be a great beginning for the shift.

The briefing room was beside the weight/exercise room and the retractable wall made it easy to hear everything that was said in either. I sat in the weight room, listening to Howard read through the lookouts and assignments, which he dispensed with quicker than usual.

When he announced that there was a new rule, concerning uniform wear, that he would be reading, the room fell completely silent. Howard began by talking about hair length and styles for both male and female officers, which sounded more than reasonable and brought a minimum of comment.

Next he highlighted the portion pertaining to tie clasps by saying only gold tie clasps and/or tie tacks would be permitted in order to compliment the gold collar emblems and badges. Also, officers would only be allowed to wear gold watches with matching band, or gold watches with black leather bands. The first grumbles started.

Howard went on. "Male officers will be required to wear only white or blue underwear in the boxer or brief cut. Female officers will also be required to wear only white or blue panties, and bikini style will be permitted. However, garter-belts, thongs and crotch-less panties are strictly prohibited and shall not be worn with the uniform under any circumstance."

This opened the door for a few comments, such as, "Is this a joke?" One male officer said it was okay with him if certain female officers wore thongs or crotch-less panties. "How can they tell me what color underwear I hafta wear?"

Howard continued. "In so far as it pertains to this portion of the order, members from the Office of Staff Inspections and Internal Affairs will conduct unannounced inspections of all male and female officers, to ensure that the rule is being strictly adhered to."

Now the rafters were rocking.

"Bullshit. You mean somebody's gonna tell me to drop my pants so they can see what color underwear I've got on?"

Others were saying the order was just a joke, but some swore by God that every word of it was true. Two officers became engaged in such a heated debate as to the order's authenticity, they wagered a steak dinner at the Sir Walter Raleigh Restaurant.

Hours later, when it was finally determined that the order was a joke, one officer was calling another to tell him how he wanted his steak cooked.

Columbia Mall Christmas

During the Christmas Season many years gone by, Herman Charity and I were assigned to work the Columbia Mall as a part of the police department's efforts to curb crime during the holidays. In about a week, store owners, managers and employees were familiar with us and welcomed our presence. Of course, in a matter of days, we saw many doors of opportunity opening for us to entertain our perverted sense of humor.

In no time at all the mall Santa came to recognize us and that's when the game began.

We waited for a child to be seated on his lap, whispering all those Christmas wishes to the dear old man and then flip him the finger from the level above his perch. The first time we caught him unaware, we thought the complete surprise of our act was going to knock him off his chair. Of course, there was nothing he could do to retaliate, and we soon made it a practice to nail him several times a night. We would appear at the railing on the second level, look down and smile at the "Jolly Old Elf" who would give a slight shake of his head, knowing he was about to get the bird. We'd flip him off, laugh and continue our rounds.

Our game of taunt Santa had gone on for at least two weeks, when our Saturday assignment was switched to daytime hours.

Herman and I arrived at the mall and began walking store to store to inform managers and employees that we'd be there all day.

As we approached the stairway near Woodward and Lothrop we heard someone yell, "Hey."

We looked up and there was Santa, standing on the stairs. Indeed this was his moment of triumph and there in his bright red suit he stood, boldly holding up his white gloved hands and giving us the finger. "You no good pricks," he yelled, "I've been waiting for this."

Herman and I laughed, figuring he was entitled to gloat and enjoy his brief time of glory, for shortly he'd have a kid on his lap and we'd nail his Santa ass again.

Maternity Notice

While working the Columbia Mall over the Christmas season, Herman and I often discovered new ways to rip off or antagonize co-workers and friends. Of course, my mind went into overdrive when we walked into the Motherhood Maternity Shop to introduce ourselves and tell the workers about our assignment.

When the Christmas season was over I asked the manager if she would give me a few envelopes and some stationary from the store. She asked why and immediately became a willing conspirator in my warped plot to play a little joke on someone. Of course, this would require zeroing in on the perfect target for such a prank, but after a little thinking there was only one obvious choice.

There was a Maryland State Trooper who took great pride in his appearance and could have easily been on recruitment posters for every branch of the military and police agency in America. He was the not a hair out of place, always look your best, regardless of the circumstance, smile at every woman you meet kind of guy and could have easily had the lead role in American Gigolo. Needless to say, he had no problems lining up dates and Pete Edge often said he wished he would throw some of his used ones his way.

For the purpose of this tale, I believe calling him Trooper First Class Gigolo would be very appropriate.

The following letter was mailed to him at the Waterloo State Police Barrack:

> *Dear Mr. Gigolo,*
>
> *On February 4th, Mary Ellen Wilson stopped by our store at the Columbia Mall and purchased three maternity dresses. At the time of purchase she informed us that you would be paying the balance of $249.95 by March 31st.*
>
> *You may pay the balance by check, money order, credit card or cash.*
>
> *We look forward to seeing you soon.*
>
> *Thank you and best wishes.*
>
> *Sincerely,*
>
> *The Girls at Motherhood Maternity Shops*

A few days after mailing the letter and while on a foot patrol of the Columbia Mall, I stopped by Motherhood Maternity Shop. Almost immediately the manager began laughing and called me aside.

She said that earlier in the day she had received a telephone call from TFC Gigolo asking about the letter and balance owed on the dresses. She told me she tried to explain that it was only a joke being played by some of his "good friends" in the Howard County Police Department, but had the feeling that he didn't really believe her.

The following night, Terry Read and I were headed out for a

little bar hoping and I met TR at his apartment. He was aware of the letter and I told him that it had been delivered and the reaction from Gigolo. He laughed and we decided to give him a call to see if he'd mention the letter.

TR called while I listened from on an extension in another room. Try as he might, TR couldn't get him to give even a vague hint of the letter or anything new happening in his life. When he went to answer a knock at this door, TR said, "What should I do?"

"Ask him if he knows Mary Ellen Wilson," I said.

When he picked up the phone again, TR asked, "Hey, do you know some chick named Mary Ellen…"

"You no good, rotten son-of-a-bitch," he yelled. "Fuck you. I even called the store."

I cut in from the extension and after TR and I had a very good laugh, I told him I drafted and sent the letter. He seemed okay with the explanation and TR and I left it at that, guessing that that was the end of it.

I returned to work the evening shift a day or two later, and immediately after I called in service the dispatcher said, "Unit 501, prepare to copy a message."

"Go ahead."

"TFC Gigolo wants you to meet him at the Columba Mall by the Hecht Company."

A few minutes later I pulled up beside his car and, before I could say a word, he said, "Jimmy, is this Motherhood Maternity Shop letter really a joke?"

I laughed. "Yes, it's a joke. The store manager told you it was a joke. TR and I told you it was a joke. I even told you I wrote the letter and sent it to the barrack. Why the hell are you so worried about it?"

"Well, back in August I was assigned to help you guys with traffic control after one of the concerts at Merriweather. By the time the assignment was over, I only had about 45 minutes left 'til the end of shift. So, I decided to pull over here on the mall lot to finish my paperwork and wait for midnight.

"A minute or so after I pulled on the lot, a car drove up and this really hot lookin' chick started talkin' to me. The next thing I knew she was giving me her address and telling me to stop by at the end of my shift. So, I went by and ended up spending the night. When I got the letter about paying the bill at Motherhood Maternity Shop, I thought it might be her."

"You mean her name is Mary Ellen Wilson?" I said, thinking I'd pulled off a one in a million joke.

"That's just it," he said, shaking his head. "I can't remember what the hell her name was?"

Bits and Pieces

Contributions from many

The Bank Robbery

In a "rare" moment of unmatched brilliance, a man intent on robbing a bank wrote out his holdup note to present to the teller. I can only imagine her expression when he shoved the note to her and she read:

"Stay CLAM I have a gun."

BOLO FOR A RUNAWAY

It was a Sunday evening when the police dispatcher alerted officers and gave the following message:

"All units, be on the lookout for the following runway in the Ellicott City area." After providing the name he broadcast, "The subject is a white male, 15 years of age. He's five feet six inches tall and weighs approximately 125 pounds. He was last seen wearing blue jeans, black tennis shoes, a dark blue jacket and a German Shepherd wearing a yellow shirt."

My immediate response, "Dispatch, can you clarify that he's wearing a German Shepherd, or does he have a German Shepherd with him that's wearing a yellow shirt?"

Driving Misbehavior

"Dispatch to any unit in the area of southbound Route One in the vicinity of Route 32, check for an "erotic" driver."

The driver was not located.

Training Day

A number of training scenarios, involving building searches for armed suspects, were arranged at the old Daniels Textile Mill.

During one of the Saturday morning exercises, SWAT Team member, Tom Sullivan was handing out equipment to officers as they prepared for training.

He was quickly passing items around saying to each officer, "Here, you take this."

With the early hour, it seemed no one was really paying attention to what Tommy was passing around. At least not until he turned to Officer Frank Dawson and said, "You take the rope."

Without looking, Frank took the black nylon "rope" and a few seconds later noted that the "rope" was moving. In an instant he discovered that he was holding a live, very long black snake.

Some swear that Frank shot straight into the air like a rocket, reaching an incredible height and letting go of the snake at the same time, while shouting a string of obscenities. Frank hit the ground running north, the snake went south and everyone else scattered to all points of the compass.

Two for One

The night shift, one very large, deceased, black snake and devious minds opened the door for mischief.

John Yeager and Bruce Lohr decided it would be fun to put the snake in Sergeant Dick Middleton's police car. They carefully wrapped the reptile around the police radio and draped the head over the mic and went to briefing, gloating over their deed.

Dick had a stack of paperwork to complete and was one of

the last out to begin his tour. He got into his car and was driving off the lot when he reached for the mic to call in service. As his hand neared the mic he drove under one of the overhead lights on the parking lot and that's when he saw the snake.

I was on the upper lot and heard someone yelling and soon realized that it was Dick Middleton calling for someone to help him. I hurried to the lower lot, burst out laughing and damn near wrecked my car.

All four doors on Middleton's cruiser were open and he was standing by the passenger's door jabbing something in and out of the car. His arms looked like pistons, pumping back and forth so fast that I couldn't tell what he had in his hands. A moment later I saw that he was poking at the snake with a 2x4 that was close to eight feet in length. To this day, I have no idea where he got the 2x4, but it certainly wasn't in the trunk of his cruiser.

I hurried over and told him he was beating a dead snake and it was okay to take it out of the car. That's when he confessed that he was terrified of snakes and wouldn't touch it. I removed the snake from the patrol car while Dick stood at least 30 feet away and watched.

After I carried the "deceased" across the parking lot and dropped it, I walked back to where Dick was standing.

"I know who did this," he said. "It was Yeager and Lohr. I knew they were up to something the way they acted during briefing."

He laughed—not exactly a happy laugh. One of those, "I'm going to get your asses for this" kind of laughs.

In no time at all, he'd come up with a devious scheme to get even with Yeager and Lohr. He picked up the mic, called and told them to meet him at the church on Route 108 just off of Route 29.

He parked his assigned cruiser and loaded his personal gear into another car, but took his time doing so. He called in service, making sure to emphasize the fact that he was driving another car.

Minutes later he was telling Yeager and Lohr, "I know you put the snake in my car. Well, I have a fear of snakes and when I saw it, I lost control of my cruiser, went up over the curb and hit a light pole. There's substantial damage to the car and I've already reported the incident to IAD. Both of you will be facing serious disciplinary action for causing me to have the accident, and you'll probably hafta pay for the damage to the car."

It wasn't until the following morning that Yeager and Lohr, after seeing Dick's undamaged assigned cruiser on the parking lot, realized that Dick Middleton had turned the tables on them. They admitted that they'd worried the entire night over the list of charges they'd be facing at the end of the shift.

Beach Preparation

Howard County Police Dispatcher, Jim Long was looking forward to a few days at the beach. He took his car to one of the local carwashes and spent extra time making sure it was sparkling inside and out.

When the job was done, he put the top down and drove off the lot, mingling with the late morning traffic.

He said, "At the first traffic light I reached across the seat, picked up a bottle of Sun-In and spritzed my hair. That's when I noticed almost immediately that a few people were staring at me. I wondered if they were jealous because they knew I was going to the beach.

"At the next traffic light I decided to spritz my hair once more. And, there they were, staring again. I couldn't believe it. I mean you'd think they never saw somebody spray a little Sun-In on their hair.

"About three traffic lights later, I reached over, grabbed the bottle and began spraying. Now, it was an entirely different group gawking and with very questionable looks on their faces. I glanced to my right and burst out laughing. My bottle of Sun-In had rolled across the seat and at each traffic light I had been spritzing my hair with Armor All."

Think Before You Boast

Howard County Police Detective Chuck Dittman told a burglary suspect, "We have your fingerprints at the crime scene."

The suspect replied, "Yeah, well, you can't prove I did all the others, because I was wearing gloves when I did them."

The Not So Great Escape

A series of armed robberies had occurred at the WaWa Store in the Swansfield area of Columbia, Maryland and left store clerks and local residents very uneasy.

The suspect, obviously the same in each instance, did little to change his appearance from one robbery to the next. He always wore blue jeans, a long tan jacket over a blue shirt and a nylon stocking pulled over his face to disguise his features and displayed a weapon described as a black, long barrelled revolver. And, he always fled in the same direction.

During one of the robberies something must have rattled him, because he grabbed the bag contained the money from the register and bolted for the door. This time, however, he didn't turn to his right to take his normal path to freedom. He sprinted straight across the grass in the direction of an apartment complex. Not long after reaching top speed he ran headlong into a chain-link fence.

One witness said, "It looked like he hit a trampoline."

His forward progress halted rather suddenly and the force of the impact hurled him backward several steps. He fell to the ground, dropping his gun and the bag with the proceeds from the robbery. It took a few seconds for him to recover, gather his gun and bag and flee toward his usual path of escape.

The following evening I knocked at his door and informed him I had a warrant for his arrest.

He played the dumb and innocent role, claiming he knew absolutely nothing about an armed robbery and didn't even know where the WaWa store was located. He ranted that the charge was bullshit and there was no evidence to connect him to the robbery.

The color began draining from his face when I said, "Well, early this morning a large brown paper bag was found in the wooded area behind Tilbury Woods. That's where you stopped to change clothes after the robbery. Inside that bag there was a pair of blue jeans, a blue shirt, a long tan jacket, a nylon stocking, and a black, long barrelled revolver (which was actually a pellet gun). Your fingerprints were found on the gun and the bag."

At that point it looked like he wanted to puke. So, I couldn't resist sticking the dagger in and giving it one final twist. "And you were kind enough to leave your driver's license in the bag."

Star Witness

Mike Chapman began his law enforcement career with the Howard County, Maryland, Police Department, eventually moving on and retiring from the DEA. Later, Mike was elected Sheriff of Loudon County, Virginia.

It was during the late 70s, while Mike was still with the Howard County PD, that he was called to investigate a hit and run accident. During the course of his investigation he learned that there were possible eyewitnesses to the collision and began attempting to locate them.

Mike had earned a reputation as an officer who pursued each and every lead and a man who refused to surrender pursuit of every possible clue. In the case of the hit and run, he was not having much luck locating even a single witness. Still, he wasn't going to give up and admit to the victim that he'd failed.

Word of Mike's relentless efforts soon reached the ears of Dispatcher Jim Long.

Jimmy said, "I hate to see Mike fail. I think he should talk to at least one witness."

Sometime after 3:00 AM, Jimmy called Mike over the police radio informing him that a witness to his hit and run had phoned and wanted to speak with him immediately.

Mike took down the number, went to the nearest telephone and called.

It was immediately apparent that, in his rush to speak with any witness to the accident, he did not hear or understand what the person answering his call had said. He identified himself and told the man who answered that he was calling to speak to an eyewitness to his hit and run investigation. After a brief explanation of the facts pertaining to his accident investigation he said, "I was told that an eye witness, a Mr. Carter, called and asked that I return his call immediately."

There was a brief pause before the man said, "You were told to call Mr. Carter at this number because he's a witness to a hit and run accident?"

"Yes, sir," Mike replied.

"You're sure of that?"

"Yes, sir."

There was another pause and then he said, "This is the White House and I don't believe President Carter witnessed your hit and run."

Ham for the Family

In the early 70s a deli known for its outstanding sandwiches and excellent cuts of various luncheon meats was open for business at the Wilde Lake Village Green in Columbia, Maryland. Its window display was truly eye catching and inviting, with its main attraction being a large ham suspended from the ceiling in the center of the display. The display was lighted day and night for all to see.

It was the ham that caught the eye of one of the locals and a regular in the crowd that made the area in and around the village center its hangout.

Night after night he would walk by the deli and apparently fantasize about what a great family meal the ham would make. At last he gave in to temptation and kicked the window, shattering the glass and grabbing the ham. He sprinted away with his prize and soon found that he had cut his ankle and leg so badly that he would require medical attention.

While he hurried to the hospital to have his wounds treated, Howard County Police arrived on the scene, discovered the break-in and the blood trail left by the suspect.

They too hurried to the hospital, where they found the hungry young lad. Soon his father arrived at the hospital and it was at that time the son confessed that his attempt to bring home a ham for the family failed miserably. The ham was made of rubber.

The "concerned" father screamed, "You dumb bastard, the next time at least steal a real one."

Trick or Treat

"Operation Pumpkin" was a vision of Lt. Garth Davis and would be implemented on Halloween night. Its primary goal was stopping or curbing acts of vandalism throughout Howard County. All leaves were cancelled and every available officer would be covering the streets and neighborhoods of the county.

Of course, the name of the operation brought a great deal of comedic outpouring from the rank and file, but Garth took the verbal jabs and not so subtle notes, especially those comparing his head to the skin of the pumpkin, left on his desk or taped to his door in stride.

Halloween night arrived and the briefing room was bursting at the seams with men and women in blue. Standing room only was the order of the day and many of the officers were crammed into the hallway leading to the room. Sector and neighborhood assignments were given and soon the parade began of patrol cars leaving Police Headquarters in Ellicott City.

Shortly after 6:00 PM a call reporting an armed robbery in progress at the pharmacy at St. John's Plaza was dispatched. In a matter of seconds so many police officers descended upon and around the plaza, the fleeing suspects couldn't reach the getaway car. The waiting driver was apprehended immediately and the "runners" covered only about 100 yards of ground before being captured.

And, the statement of the day from one of the suspects, "Who the fuck told us there no cops in Howard County?"

Barely two hours old and "Operation Pumpkin" was already declared a success. The remainder of the evening would seem boring compared to its beginning, but the vandals were appearing.

Officer Larry Horn was on the hunt for a car occupied by at least four teens that were hurling eggs at homes, cars and trick or treating children. He drove up and down the streets of Valley Mede determined to find them. For over two hours he always seemed to be one street away or just missing one of their deeds. But, Larry wasn't a man who gave up on a quest.

It was getting late and the pedestrian traffic was becoming non-existent and Larry was beginning to fear that he wouldn't find the "egg bandits" as he called them. But a left turn on to Brookmede Road and the car was in front of him. He turned on the overhead lights and stopped the car, chuckling to himself and muttering, "Got you little pricks."

He ordered the four teenaged boys out of the car and told them to "assume the position" on the passenger's side of the car. They didn't say a word, but put their hands on the roof of the car and hung their heads.

Larry began searching the car and later said, "I was gonna look in the back first and I 'accidently' stepped on three cartons of eggs that were on the floor. I tried to be careful, but my foot slipped three or four times and crushed the damn things flat. Then I saw a carton of eggs on the front seat and I took it out and tried to put it on the roof of the car. The carton must've been defective because all the eggs fell out and broke on the windshield."

Satisfied that no more eggs were in the car, Larry turned his attention to the boys. As they stood up to face him he noticed very strange bulges in the pockets of their jeans and the sleeves of their shirts. He began tapping their pockets with his nightstick and heard a cracking sound and he said, "You know, I heard the same thing when I tapped on their shirt sleeves. So, I thought I'd better check their socks. Wouldn't you know it? They had the same bulges in their socks. Tap, tap, tap and they disappeared."

The boys stood there and stared at him, probably thinking that even after having their eggs scrambled, they were going to be arrested. But, Larry said, "Okay, boys, you can go."

"You mean you aren't gonna arrest us," the driver said.

"No. I don't think you have any more eggs."

With that, one of the boys stepped forward and held out his hand, showing him one egg. "You want this one, Officer?"

Larry took his nightstick, smacked the egg and said, "Nah, you keep it."

"Operation Pumpkin" closed a big success with only minor incidents of vandalism reported and four armed robbers lamenting their visit to Howard County.

Stationhouse Lust

Don Bathgate was an easy-going man who I often called the very first Community Police Officer. Wherever he worked, in no time at all, he seemed to know every businessman and woman on his beat, and he knew every troublemaker as well. Big, strong and soft-spoken would be a good description of Don, which seemed to attract many female admirers. More than one woman, young and old, said he made their heart flutter.

One of the female employees at the Howard County Police Department found PFC Don Bathgate to be the man of her dreams, or at least her lustful fantasies. Early on, she made it a point to cast a casual hint on two in his direction each time she saw him. But, he chose to ignore the comments and go on his way.

As time passed, the hints became laced with a bit of sexual overtone, but Don let them pass as if nothing had been said. This only encouraged her, and she became bolder with her suggestions at every opportunity. And, still, there was no response from Don.

Then on a day when Don arrived early for the evening shift, she decided to challenge him. Standing a few feet away, with a half-dozen other officers between them, she opened fire. "Well, Donald, I think you ignore me because you're afraid of it."

He laughed and very calmly replied, "No, I'm not. I've been through the harbor tunnel before."

Signs and Bumper Stickers

Throughout the years many signs and bumper stickers have appeared on personally owned vehicles as well as the marked and unmarked police cars.

One police dispatcher hurried away from her evening shift and began driving to her home in Baltimore. Along the way, Ranae noticed that she was, at first, getting a few strange looks, a number of smiles and thumps up and an increasing number of catcalls and whistles. When she reached the city limits, she began getting a number of lewd and suggestive comments and, soon, the outright propositions were being offered. She was confused by the bizarre happenings as she had travelled the same route for months and never encountered such behavior.

She parked her car near her home and, as she passed between the front of her car and the back of another, she found the reason for the X-rated taunts.

Taped squarely between the headlights of her car was a very large sign, which read: RENT ME.

***

Detective Bob Myers set out in the early morning hours and drove to Baltimore City, with warrant in hand, in search of a felony suspect.

He spoke with cab drivers and truck drivers, police officers and deputy sheriffs, but was having no luck locating his suspect. As the day wore on, he noticed these same cab and truck drivers, police and sheriffs were casting some very questioning glances his way. But, he soon realized that almost everyone was giving him a puzzled look. He shrugged and continued his quest, finally giving up and returning to Howard County.

Later that evening, Bob changed into his workout gear and went out for a run. He walked to back of his police car and, as he was putting his foot on the bumper to tie his shoe, he saw the bumper sticker.

Affixed squarely in the center of the bumper, printed in bold lime green letters on a black background, the altered bumper sticker read: WARNING – I BRAKE FOR NAKED MEN.

CID Wars

The battle of wits and outlandish scheming became a never-ending crusade between several detectives in the Howard County Police Department's Criminal Investigations Bureau as they duelled to outdo the other in the humor and pranks arena.

It was said that Bob Myers opened the doors to the game when he called the Baltimore City Police Department where Detective Carl Layman was attending a training session. He lured a secretary into becoming a co-conspirator in his scheme and she walked into the classroom and announced for all to hear, "Detective Layman, your AIDS test came back negative."

While Carl was attending the class, Bob and Detective Pat Full found his newly printed batch of business cards. About a dozen or more of the cards were removed from the box and messages, such as, "I tested positive for AIDS, I'd love to date your daughter, I'd love to date your son, I'd like to date you, please call, I had sex with your cat, and I enjoy sex with goats" were typed on the backs of the cards. Bob and Pat then placed them randomly in the box with the others, hoping an unsuspecting Carl would hand them out.

When Carl returned from the training session he vowed to take the fight to Bob. He talked with Pat Full and she very quickly decided to play on both sides of the battle. She handed over a booklet filled with every imaginable sex toy and gag gift on the market. And, of course, she had removed the booklet from Bob's desk.

A week or so later he arrived for work, sat down at his desk and nearly fell out of his chair laughing. He had a large coffee cup on his desk that was filled with dozens of pens and pencils. Only today each and every pen and pencil was adorned with an eraser in the shape of a penis head. He suspected immediately that they'd been ordered from the booklet in his desk and hurriedly began thumbing through the pages. He soon discovered the advertisement for "Little Pecker Pencil Tops" and pointed a finger at Layman.

The war of words and accusations over the "Little Pecker Pencil Tops" was in overdrive when Officer Kevin Meile of the SWAT team walked into the office. In a matter of seconds he was caught up in the laughter and finger pointing over the "erasers" and joked about putting some on the pens of his fellow SWAT team members.

The joking, accusations and "useful" suggestions for the erasers were going to warp speed as other detectives arrived for work. Pens and pencils were modelled in various shirts and suit coats and one was crudely attached as a lapel pin, while Kevin checked to see how they went with his uniform.

Kevin finally remembered that he'd stopped by the office to gather information on a group of robbery suspects that were hitting the Baltimore and Howard County area. In a brief moment of order, he picked up a lookout sheet and left to meet with other members of the tactical team.

They met at a Roy Rogers Restaurant in Ellicott City to eat and plan the evening's surveillance strategy.

While placing his order, Kevin noticed that the young lady behind the counter seemed occupied with something other than what he wanted to eat. He paused in mid order and realized that she was staring at his shirt and it looked as if she was desperately struggling to hold back a laugh.

He looked down to see what she was staring at and instantly saw two "Little Pecker Pencil Tops" protruding from the pen pocket of his uniform shirt. Turning a deep crimson, he grabbed the pens and pulled them out of his pocket as the young lady lost control and burst into a fit of laughter.

The Paint Test

For years the Maryland State Highway Department had been testing the durability of paints, which were used to mark the roads with center and edge lines. Utilizing a section of U. S. Route 40 in Ellicott City, they painted lines of bright yellow and white, which stretched across the concrete surface from edge line to edge line in the East and West bound lanes.

A sign was posted to signal drivers and read: PAINT TEST DRIVE NORMALLY.

At some unknown time and date in the mid to late 1960s a police officer stopped what he determined to be a suspicious vehicle. The stop was made on U. S. Route 40 in the area of the painted lines. The driver asked why he was stopped and the officer immediately replied that he'd failed the paint test.

No Howard County Police Officer or Maryland State Trooper

admitted to being the first to stop someone for failing the paint test. It was, however, widely used for many years thereafter as the reason for traffic stops in that area of Route 40.

Over time, Officer Griff Jones was given credit as the very first to employ that reason for a traffic stop. If indeed, Griff was the first to use that excuse for a traffic stop, it should be noted that after stopping a car for failing the paint test, he met the young woman he would later marry.

Griff and Betty have now been married for over 50 years.

The Mail Must Go Through

There are times when good old fashion common sense should take priority over "Neither rain, nor snow, nor gloom of night…" or whatever that entire slogan happens to be for the postal department.

It was snow, sleet and freezing rain falling on the parking lot and exits of the Normandy Shopping Center in Ellicott City that turned them into a skating rink. One exit, a very steep hill, which was at least a quarter mile in length and intersected Rogers Avenue at its bottom, became a sheet of ice in no time.

Officer Fred McHargue was dispatched to the shopping area and told to block the exit at the top of the hill. He quickly found that standing was as much a problem as driving, but dutifully stood his post after parking his cruiser and activating the overhead lights.

At some point a U. S. Mail delivery truck rounded a corner and approached the intersection. Fred began waving to the driver and directing him away from the intersection, but he didn't see or chose to ignore Fred's signals.

He drove around the police car and shouted out the window to Fred, "The mail must go through."

A second later he hit the ice at the top of hill and, at this time "Oh, shit" would have been an understatement. The truck began sliding sideways, then made a number of 360 degree turns, and soon began bouncing from curb to curb, all the while picking up speed and heading for the intersection at the bottom of the hill.

The driver's intention was altered, but the mail certainly did go through—through the exit at the bottom, across Rogers Avenue, over the curb and through the scrubs at the entrance to Town and Country Apartments.

The results and recommendations of the U.S. Postal Service's investigation were never revealed to the police department. Although it became a joke among officers that the driver had probably been reassigned and was delivering mail by dogsled in Nome, Alaska.

Hot Pursuit

Police codes have been a part of the job for as long as most can remember, but in the 70s the code system went to a level beyond comprehension. One set of codes ranged from 10-0 to 10-99 and the other numbered codes designated a specific crime—a Code One was a murder, Code Two, Rape, Code Three, Armed Robbery and so on up the ladder.

An officer working Western Howard County made a traffic stop late on a Friday afternoon. After the stop he ran a wanted check on the driver and a few minutes later the dispatcher replied that the man was 10-99 for a Code 33 violation. That translated to the man being wanted for being AWOL from the military. He placed the man under arrest and called for a tow truck to impound his car. He put the arrestee in the back seat of his cruiser, but did not seatbelt him as required.

Not long after that he was told to bring the suspect to police headquarters immediately after the tow truck arrived. That was not the normal protocol, which was to remain with the tow truck driver until he secured the car and began the drive to the impound lot.

When the tow truck arrived, the officer took it upon himself to disobey the order, got out of his car and walked to meet the tow truck driver. Soon, the usual socializing began and the prisoner was forgotten. In the blink of an eye the friendly bullshit session went to hell.

The officer and the tow truck driver watched the police car making a very rapid U-Turn and then take off at a very high rate of speed southbound on Route 97 with the handcuffed prisoner behind the wheel.

Soon thereafter the comedy hour began with the tow truck in

hot pursuit of the stolen police car. The driver of the truck was doing his best to catch up while the officer stood on the running board on the passenger's side of the truck, clinging to the mirror and probably praying for divine intervention.

The police car was abandoned at the intersection of Route 97 and Burntwoods Road and the prisoner escaped into the fields of a nearby farm.

As it turned out the improper code was given to the officer and the man was wanted for a Code Three, Armed Robbery not a Code 33, AWOL. That was the reason for the order to bring the prisoner directly to the station and forego the social hour with the tow truck operator. But, the code correction was not given at the time of the order.

The suspect was captured after a two-day search and the officer, after a bit of "coaching" decided that a career move was in order and resigned from the department.

Vending Machine Surprises

A number of vending machines were located on the lower level of the police station, with offerings from cigarettes to candy and apples. One particular vending machine gave those of us with demented minds an opportunity for fun and games.

The "fun" machine offered various selections with prices ranging from 40 cents to $1.25. There were apples, cakes, pies and other items that, with a push of a button, rotated from left to right until the selection desired came into view. With that, you inserted the proper amount of money and opened the thick plastic door on the far right-hand side of the machine to retrieve your purchase. Once the door was opened, however, it would not lock until the button was pushed again to begin the rotation process. Of course, it wasn't long before this was discovered and soon the games began.

The first item to appear in the machine was an apple with a large bite taken from the fruit. A banana peel, a mug shot of one of our local criminals, a light bulb, a small Styrofoam replica of a civil war cannon, which looked more like a penis with testicles attached, and a miniature diploma indicating the recipient had graduated with a Master of Arts Degree from a local college were a few of the items placed in the vending machine.

One vending machine tech was obviously as demented as the police officers and often moved the items placed in the machine to locations with higher or lower prices. He admitted that he looked forward to his stop at the police station because he never knew what he'd find. Naturally, that thought held true for everybody.

A new dispatcher was hired and arrived for the day shift and given a quick tour of the building. About mid-morning he asked if he could go to the lower level to get something from the vending machines and was sent on his way.

A few minutes later he returned to the radio room looking quite baffled. When asked what was wrong he shook his head and said, "There's a clam in one of the vending machines."

Jody Tookey replied, "Don't worry about it. All kinds of things show up in those machines. It's no big surprise to hear that there's a clam in one."

He shrugged and said, "Yeah, but this one has blue eyes and a beard."

Tis the Season

Christmas was only days away and those of us assigned to the HCPD Crime Lab were joking about Santa's upcoming visit and wondering aloud if any of us would really make his "Nice" list.

While accusations of perceived misbehavior were tossed about the room, one officer seemed preoccupied. He was quietly toiling over something on his desk and avoiding the verbal joust, although he did laugh from time to time over some of the barbs that were flying back and forth. Finally, he got up from his desk and chuckled.

Some months prior, an L shaped segment of wood ended up in the office. It had no evidence tag and no lab request for any type of processing. So, it was put aside and forgotten.

It was a strange looking object, which measured about one-quarter inch wide, with the bottom portion of the L being about 8 to

10 inches in length and the other about 28 inches. At the time it was dropped in the lab it had a string of very small white lights that ran the length of both segments, with exposed wires only at one end.

Now, the lights were working. Officer Genius had somehow found a way to get them to operate by using a battery. The tiny white bulbs lighted in sequence, beginning at the base of the longer segment and ending at the tip of the other. If you followed the lights as they began their trek from one end to the other, you suddenly found that they drew your attention to a portion of mistletoe that had been attached at the shorter base.

At first, our resident genius tried to find a way to attach the longer segment to his back and have the shorter piece above and mistletoe dangling over his head. His intention, naturally, was to stroll casually around the station in hopes of stealing a Christmas kiss or two from willing young ladies. Alas, he was unable to get his invention attached to his back.

Well, that didn't deter his thinking and scheming. About 20 minutes later he had reworked his creation and proudly announced it ready for testing. When he turned around to display his work of art, all of us damn near fell out of our chairs laughing.

The lights were in perfect working order, flowing in precise sequence and drawing attention to the mistletoe, which now hung directly over the zipper of his uniform trousers.

He laughed and said, "I wonder if I can get a little kiss for Santa's Trouser Trout."

To which someone replied, "If you get caught wandering the halls by somebody from the Command Staff, you could find yourself in the unemployment line, clutching Santa's very limp Trouser Trout in your hand."

Main Street Wine Night

Main Street Ellicott City had its share of local "bad asses." When alcohol became a part of the mix, bad asses always seemed to sprout bigger muscles, more combative attitudes and were always ready to challenge the police officer on the beat.

One such individual, I'll call Cecil, was standing on the

corner of Main Street and Maryland Avenue on a Friday evening, sipping from a bottle of some state's finest 99 cent wine.

It wasn't long before a call came into the radio room from a concerned citizen reporting the offense. A moment later an officer was dispatched to check for the violation and take the appropriate enforcement action.

The officer sent to meet Cecil had been a Baltimore City Officer for some years before accepting a lateral transfer to Howard County. He parked his squad car, got out, approached Cecil and informed him of the no drinking in public laws and told him to take his bottle inside.

Cecil, alcohol infused muscles and attitude at their peak, said, "Fuck you, I'll drink where I want," and raised the bottle to his lips.

In a flash the officer's nightstick snapped up and sliced the bottle in half.

Cecil, clutching the bottle and looking totally bewildered by the officer's actions, pointed the remnants at him.

The officer said, "Oh, threatening an officer with a deadly weapon," and promptly knocked him unconscious.

Cecil was cuffed, dragged to the police car and stuffed in the back seat for a ride to the station. There, he was dragged from the car, through the middle of the in-progress night shift briefing and to the holding cell area.

A prisoner, who had already been brought in for lodging, took offense to the way Cecil was being treated. He grabbed the bars of his cell, spat at the officer and screamed, "You fuckin' pig, you can't treat my friend that way."

A fist shot up between the bars and landed squarely on the chin of the offended prisoner. He staggered back about three steps and collapsed.

The Friday Night Wine and Bad Attitude Fest were declared officially over.

Sanity Check

A call went out to Bob Myers and another officer to respond to Howard County General Hospital and meet with doctors in the ER regarding a patient. Shortly after arrival they found that they would be taking the patient to Springfield State Hospital in Sykesville for a mental evaluation.

Doctors were still in the process of completing the required paperwork and the senior officer directed Myers to take the patient to his car, while he remained behind to wait for the packet.

Myers escorted the patient to his patrol car and, following the department's protocol for transport, handcuffed and secured him in the back seat.

Myers got in his car, looked over his shoulder at the patient and smiled, while asking how he was. He received no response and shrugged, figuring the man didn't care to engage in conversation. At that point he reached up and removed a pair of glasses from behind the visor.

A moment later he put them on, turned and looked at the man in the backseat. The man gave him a strange look, but said nothing. Suddenly, Myers removed the glasses, grabbed a cloth and began vigorously rubbing as though attacking some foreign substance on his glasses. Seconds later he stopped, put the glasses on and looked back at the patient again. This time the man leaned forward and stared at Bob, who quickly pulled off the glasses. Now, he held them up toward the windshield, pulled them back and began blowing on them. He tapped them on the dash, put them on and glanced over his shoulder at the man, who now seemed baffled by his actions. All of a sudden Bob had the glasses off, tapping them on the dash, pulling them back and blowing on them before giving another very quick dusting motion with the cloth. This time after putting them on, he saw the officer coming out of the ER door with the paperwork and started the engine.

The officer got into the passenger's seat and said, "Let's go."

Bob looked over, smiled and said, "Yes, sir."

Instantly the officer saw that the "glasses" Myers wore were simply frames without lenses. "When we get to Springfield maybe you should stay there with this guy."

A What in Progress

The sound of the emergency tone booming over the radio and followed by a report of a crime in progress gets the adrenalin rushing and the heart racing. So it was on a sunny afternoon when the radio dispatcher was calling for any officer in the area of Wilde Lake to respond to a rape in progress. The dispatcher continued, saying that a woman could see the attack taking place from a window in her apartment behind the lake.

No less than a half-dozen officers called to say they were on the way to the crime scene. Naturally, the adrenalin was rushing on to overdrive as the dispatcher announced that the attack was still going on and the parties were engaged in a violent struggle.

Officers leaving the police station to begin their tour of duty were now responding as well. And, the dispatcher said the witness was telling her that the assault was still ongoing.

By now, officers closing in on the scene are certain they are going to catch a rapist before he can flee the area. One officer calls that he is out of his car in front of the woman's apartment building. In a matter of seconds he is running, gun in hand, around the corner of the building and toward the lake. Now, behind the building he stops and scans the area around the lake, but sees no suspect fleeing and hears no screams.

A sliding glass door behind him opens and a woman runs out, pointing and yelling. "There! There! Over there!"

An angry voice screams over the radio, "Headquarters, have all responding units cancel. The rape in progress is two Mallard ducks fornicating."

It seems the Mallard mating ritual appeared quite violent to the complaining party. Thus, the call for a rape in progress.

The Good, The Bad and The Funny

Ed Puls

Tending the Garden

While working in Forensic Services/Crime Lab I learned early on that searching for and collection of evidence often requires going above, and sometimes below, the call of duty. The above isn't so bad, but the below—well, that can be downright bad and really ugly. I've gone from rooftops to storm drains and, yes, even down into the sewer drains to retrieve evidence.

Yet, every now and then, something comes along that has a way of brightening your day.

On a relatively warm spring day, Sergeant Lilley had us out behind an apartment complex in Columbia searching for evidence related to a robbery. While I was walking along, looking back and forth, I noticed several flowerpots sitting side by side about 60 to 70 feet from the rear of one of the buildings.

I smiled, guessing that someone who was taking advantage of the warm spring sunshine and getting a running start on the growing season placed them there. And, sure enough, there were almost a dozen Marijuana plants soaking up the sun. Since, we were unable to connect them directly to a particular apartment, I pulled them up and stuffed them in a plastic evidence bag. Then, taking a page from one of my favorite pranksters' book, I knew I couldn't walk away and leave the owner wondering what happened to his plants.

So, I took out one of my very official Howard County Police Department business cards and left a note.

"I know who took your plants. Call me."

I guess he didn't wanna know what happened to his plants because he never called.

Canoes, Rafts and Office Space

Often times a particular case or cases brought us together with other departments and I worked with the Maryland State Police on many cases over the years. During that time I got to know and become good friends with the Barrack Commander at Waterloo.

I happened by Waterloo one afternoon and saw him standing nose to nose with a Trooper and ripping him a new ass. It seems the Trooper, in a moment of questionable sanity, had taken a canoe and stuck it in the commander's office. Granted, the commander had a good sense of humor, but he also knew he couldn't allow this to go unpunished. To do so would open the door for the likes of Pete Edge and Donny Newcomer to declare open season on him and God only knows what that could lead to. So, the Trooper was sent away with an ass chewing and an assignment to desk duty, which almost all considered worse than being sent to jail.

Later that afternoon I drove by the barrack and noticed that the 14-foot canoe had been removed from the commander's office and placed in a storage area. Sitting beside it was a 17-foot canoe and suddenly the devil was whispering in my ear. The voice of good reason said, "Don't do it, Ed," and the devil stepped up and said, "I dare you, Ed."

Four nights later I was working a stakeout and drove through the barrack lot. I could see the Trooper serving his sentence sitting at the front desk, fighting desperately to stay alert. A quick peek and I saw the canoes were still in the storage area. The devil was back and there I was parking my car, stuffing my lock pick set in my pocket and heading for the canoes.

I picked up the 17-foot canoe and carried it to the back door of the barrack, knowing I was safe from the cameras. The barrack commander had told me over lunch a few days ago that only one was working. Repairs had been requested, but as usual, it was the old "we'll get to you when we can," response.

I put the canoe down, punched in the combination and went inside, lugging the canoe. It was a straight shot to the commander's office and a minute later I was picking the lock. Soon, I found that the canoe was only a foot shorter than the office was long and I had to lift several ceiling tiles to get it inside. It took some work, but at last I managed to get it settled in place. I was admiring my handy work when I realized that the canoe was also wedged firmly against the door. I was stuck in the office!

So, it was out the window, around the corner to my car and a fast exit from the lot.

I knew the Barrack Commander arrived for work at about the same time every day. So, the following morning I made my arrival time five minutes after his. When I walked into the barrack I could hear the commander bellowing at a Trooper, demanding to know who worked the desk on the night shift. Of course, when the night shift desk Trooper arrived, he didn't know a thing about the canoe and how it got in the office.

I thought it was time to intervene and walked down the hall, but before I could say a word the Captain turned to me and said, "Do you see what this asshole did last night?" He went on about how someone from maintenance would have to be called and the canoe cut in half to get it out.

I decided it was time to offer my expert advice on the matter and told him it looked as if the perpetrator made his escape through the window. He agreed and a minute later we were outside looking for footprints, but wouldn't you know it? There were none. But, the maintenance man arrived and saved the day, and without having to cut the canoe in half.

About two months passed and I was at the barrack again and

overheard the Quartermaster grumbling that he had to throw certain equipment away because of age or expiration. The Captain told him to quit his bitching and get rid of the stuff. As I was walking by, I saw a stack of boxes and crates being moved to the trash area and one of the crates was clearly marked, "FAA—Inflatable Raft." An instant later the devil arrived and said, "Go ahead."

It was 4:00 AM and I was long off duty when I arrived at the barrack. I parked my car and hurried to the trash area and found the FAA—Inflatable Raft still there. I looked closer at the packaging label and found the raft was marked as being rated for a capacity of seven, with an overload capacity of ten, making it a fairly large raft.

I got it out of the crate and managed to drag it to the back door of the barrack. Next, it was through the door and down the hallway to the commander's office. That's when I realized that I'd forgotten my lock pick set, but good fortune smiled—the door was unlocked. I pulled the raft into the office and closed the door.

After looking over the raft for a few minutes I decided to hook the handle that activated the raft to the doorknob. The weight of the raft would be sufficient to hold it in place and fate would take care of the rest. Out the window and I vanished into the night.

A few hours later I was back at the barrack for a meeting with the drug task force. The meeting was still in its early stages when we heard, "BAM! Sssssssssssssssssssssssss. Thump."

Then came a scream of "What the fuck was that?"

All of us hurried into the hallway where we saw the barrack commander, gun in hand, staring at his door. The bang from the raft apparently sounded like gunfire and he thought someone had shot at him from his office. A moment later he holstered his weapon and looked into his office, finding that the force of the inflating raft had moved his desk several feet. He calmly turned, walked down the hall to the front desk and told the Trooper, "My office had better be clean when I get back."

A group of us from the task force worked our way inside and removed the raft, while the Trooper straightened the office. He was just finishing up when the Captain returned.

After the meeting I dropped by the commander's office and

found that he was in a pretty good mood. He and I had been very good friends for a long time and had certainly swapped stories over mugs of cold beer and maybe a shot or two. So, he didn't have a problem confiding in me that he was absolutely sure that the canoe and raft pranksters were members of the Maryland State Police and he had a suspect or two in mind.

Well, if he was going to make it that easy for me to get off the hook, I saw no need to confess my sins. And, even with the passing of time he never learned that I was the prankster.

There was another side of the Captain that I'm sure many were unaware of. He cared deeply for those under his command and went out of his way to protect them. In that sense, I mean from baseless allegations.

He came to me and asked me to help him resolve an issue relating to one of his Troopers. The Trooper was working a part time job, as so many of us have had to do to make ends meet. A company representative met with him and accused the Trooper of stealing while working security for his corporation.

The Captain told me he didn't want to involve Internal Affairs in the matter unless it was positively necessary. In fact, he didn't want the Trooper to know such an allegation had been made against him.

In a matter of a few days of surveillance I discovered that the real thief was one of the company's managers. A search warrant was executed at his home and much of the stolen property was recovered. In the end, the Trooper never knew of the investigation and that's the way the Captain wanted it. He didn't want someone under his command knowing he'd been accused of a crime that the commander all along believed he was incapable of committing.

They don't make commanders like that anymore.

New Head Wear

Harry Wink

At a time when the department was discussing tossing out the Smokey Bear Campaign Hats and switching to new head wear there was a call for suggestions. I mentioned this to family members and friends and someone among those I had spoken to arrived at my house with their own suggestion.

They gave me a yellow helmet that had a revolving red light on the top, a chinstrap that contained a toy microphone and a siren. Of course, this was opportunity knocking and I wasn't going to pass it up.

I walked into a night shift briefing wearing the helmet, red light revolving and siren sounding, went to my seat and sat down. I turned off the siren and nodded to Lieutenant Geisler who looked as though he wasn't sure what to do. He stared at me for a few seconds and then went on with briefing, probably wondering if he should have me committed or send me out to work.

After briefing I was told to set up radar along Little Patuxent Parkway in the vicinity of the Columbia Mall because of complaints about speeding cars leaving the local watering holes. Thirty minutes later I was on post and waiting for the first client of night. That's when the challenge was thrown out by one of the officers on the stop team.

"Harry, you don't have the balls to wear that helmet on a car stop."

And, like magic, there's the first speeder of the night and I waved him over. I calmly put on the helmet, turned on the light and siren and walked up to his car. Siren off, microphone on and I said "Good evening, sir. I'm Officer Wink of the Howard County Police and I've stopped you for exceeding the posted speed limit."

His response, "Sir, why're you wearing that helmet?"

"We're testing potential new headgear, designed especially for officer safety on the night shift," I said and then promptly told him I'd only be writing a warning for the speed violation.

He took the warning, shook his head and drove off without offering an opinion on the headgear.

Late Night Snack

I was assigned to the night shift as the K-9 Officer and called to the Columbia Mall to assist officers in a search after they found an open door.

I arrived and took Schnapps out of the back and into the mall. We checked the mall top to bottom and all was secure. So, there we were standing around slinging the usual night time bullshit, when one of the officers notices the dog has slipped away.

"Hey, Harry, where's Schnapps?"

I looked around, but didn't see him. I called for him and he didn't respond, which was very unusual. So, we started looking around and calling for him, but he just wasn't responding.

At the time there were dozens of kiosks on the lower level of the mall. During business hours, the operators of the booths were selling everything from beads and purses to food. I noticed the flap on one of them was pulled aside and I started walking over to check it. As I got closer I could see Schnapps' tail. I pulled the flap open and there he was helping himself to some sausage and cheese, which very quickly had everybody laughing.

Schnapps wasn't pleased at all when I dragged his ass away from his banquet, but later on he would have his revenge. About 30 minutes after leaving the mall the sausage and cheese kicked in and he sat behind me for the rest of the night farting. To make things even worse, it started to rain and I couldn't open the windows and let the growing gas cloud escape. And, I swear, every time I looked in the rear view mirror Schnapps was grinning.

Working Radar

Being a certified radar operator often provided various forms of entertainment and greetings from community members. On the stops we meet everyone from the polite and apologetic to the very belligerent. On the other side of the coin, many have been happy to see us in their neighborhood enforcing the speed laws. On sweltering summer days those of us on their streets have been treated to pitchers of iced tea, cold lemonade and bottles of water. When the weather cooled, we were offered hot coffee or chocolate. One woman was so happy to learn that we would be running radar on her street on four consecutive mornings, she brought us a tray with hot coffee and breakfast every day.

Over the years I've had the opportunity to work with dozens of officers while assigned to speed enforcement posts. While with the First Platoon I worked frequently with Joe Ganascioli, Dave Steves and Leo Cordero. And, I knew I could always count on our supervisor, Sergeant Lilley to come by and make a few stops with us. Of course, his stopping by often provided us with a few laughs.

I always loved it when I was writing a summons and the driver said, "I demand to see your supervisor."

"Yes, sir/ma'am, that's him over there writing a summons."

"Never mind. I don't wanna talk with him."

I'll never forget the day when Jim went three for three in the belligerent driver stops.

We were working radar on Phelps Luck Drive in Columbia for the second consecutive day. The previous day went well with the old cliché "Shooting fish in a barrel," because we'd stopped and written so many drivers. So, we figured day two would be just as productive.

A car came through at 18 over and Jim was up. He waved the car over and asked the driver, a young man in his early 20s for his license and registration. The young man gave him his license and registration along with a barrage of verbal abuse.

"Man, this is fuckin' bullshit. This is harassment. You no good pricks got nothin' better to do than fuck with me. I'll see your ass in court. My lawyer's gonna take your ass apart."

Jim smiled, handed him his copy of the summons and said, "Have a nice day, sir."

In no time at all he was stepping up to the plate for his next stop. He walked up to the car and a minute later came back with the driver's license and registration. He looked at me and said, "This man's 75 years old and has his grandchildren in the car. I'm just gonna write him a warning and send him on his way."

Jim had just started to write out the warning when the man walked back and slammed his hands down on the hood of the patrol car, snarling, "Who's the son-of-a-bitch that authorized you to run radar on my street?"

Jim looked at him and said, "Well, sir, since I'm the area supervisor, I guess that makes me the son-of-a-bitch."

With that I saw him push the warning book aside and reach for his summons book and begin writing.

The man pointed to the warning book and said, "What was that?"

"That was a warning. This is a summons," he said with a smile.

"No, I'll just take the warning."

"No, sir, you won't take a warning. You'll take a summons."

Then it started.

"I'll call the county executive and have this taken care of. In fact, I'll call the governor and complain about this bullshit. I'm calling him as soon as I get home."

"Sir, you can call the Pope if you like, but you're still getting a summons."

He completed the summons, explained it to the man and told him where to sign.

"Screw you, I'm not signing your bullshit summons."

Joe Ganascioli looked over at me and laughed. "Harry, this should be good."

Jim just smiled. "Sir, if you don't sign it, you'll be arrested for refusing to sign the summons. I'll have your car impounded and I'll call Social Services and have them take your grandchildren."

"You can't arrest me."

When he saw Jim reaching for the handcuffs, he changed his mind and signed the summons. After getting his copy, he started walking back to his car mentioning all of the important people he knew and would be calling to complain.

Hit number three came up quickly when a car drove into the radar beam well over the limit. I said, "Sarge, this one's 22 over."

He stepped out, pointed to the car and waved to the driver to pull over. An instant later a woman was screaming out the window, "Fuck you! Fuck you!" She pulled the car to the curb and continued yelling, "Fuck you, I wasn't speeding. Fuck you!"

He walked to the car and very calmly said, "Good afternoon, ma'am. I'm Sergeant Lilley, Howard County Police and I'd like to have your driver's license and registration, please."

"Fuck you, I wasn't speeding."

"Ma'am, your license and registration, please."

Joe and I could see her flipping through her wallet and she was obviously going to make every effort to keep Jim waiting as long as possible. At one point I heard him say, "Ma'am, you keep passing your license. Go back and take it out."

While her string of obscenities continued to flow, I called

over to Jim. "Sarge, I wrote her yesterday for the same thing." I'm guessing that's why she was so pissed off.

Finally Jim stepped back from the car, looked over at me and said, "Do you still have the copy of your summons from yesterday?"

I held up my summons book. "Right here."

He smiled at the driver and said, "Never mind, ma'am. I'll just copy his."

With that he turned and walked back to the police car, took my summons book and began copying her information. He paused at one point and said, "Can you believe she has two children in the car with her?"

"Same yesterday, Sarge."

"Well, she's sure setting a fine example for them."

A minute later he walked back to the car and explained the summons to her, including her options of paying the fine and her right to appear in court, if she chose to do so.

She grabbed the summons book out of his hand, signed her summons and shoved it back out the window to him. Joe and I were surprised that she didn't throw it at him. Then she yelled, "Don't you have something for me?"

Again, Jim smiled, pulled her copy of the summons from the book and passed it to her. As she snatched it out of his hand he said, "Ma'am, you have a very pleasant day."

She drove about a hundred feet, pounded on the horn and flipped us the finger before she drove on.

Jim shook his head. "God, I hope that bitch comes to court," and a few seconds later he was gathering up his summons book and walking toward his car.

"Hey, Sarge, you're not leaving are you?"

"Hell, yeah. I've had about all the Columbia kindness and courtesy I can stand. In fact, I'm not sure I'll ever work radar with you guys again."

Night Shift Follies
Dave Suggs

Mark Colbert and I drove up to an old dirt road behind the county jail, where I parked my cruiser and got in Mark's car. We were sitting there talking when Ed Buckman pulled up and started talking with us.

After a few minutes we noticed that Ed was no longer a part of our conversation.

Colbert says, "That prick's asleep."

Mark had a box of Kleenex on his front seat and decided to wake Buckman up by lighting one on fire and tossing it in his car. The first one sailed in the window and went out pretty quick. So he tossed another over into Ed's car. No response. So, he kept it up, tossing one flaming Kleenex after another into Ed's car.

All of a sudden Ed's head popped up and he started yelling and beating on his chest. The last burning tissue had ignited the front of his shirt.

The "You're in deep shit" light begins flashing because the request submitted to the Quartermaster for a replacement shirt would have to provide a reason for the item being replaced.

So, now here we are trying not to laugh and, at the same time figure out a way to explain the scorch marks and the hole burned in the front of Buckman's shirt.

Ed got a new shirt after "Accidental Flare Burn" was listed on the form, but I'm not so sure the Quartermaster bought it.

My Aching Feet

Early one morning, after things quieted down, I decided to make a last minute check of my college homework. I pulled under a bank drive thru near Route 29 and 32, which was well lighted, and picked up my books to scan the assignment.

All night long my feet had been aching, probably because of the new shoes I was wearing. I don't know why, and I admit it was a dumb ass move, but I took off my shoes. So, there I am with happy feet when I heard a car coming northbound on 29—not just driving, but roaring up the highway.

"Ahhh, shit!"

I grabbed my shoes, stuffed my feet in them and took off in pursuit, calling for backup. Up 29 we go and the guy decides to exit on to Route 175. He took the ramp too fast, lost control and crashed. I jumped out of my cruiser, ran to his car and was pulling him out as Lieutenant Cogle arrived on the scene.

After things calmed down, I noticed the Lieutenant looking at me. He walked over and said, "Officer Suggs, is there any particular reason for your shoes being on the wrong feet?"

"Lieutenant, I know you're not gonna believe this, but…"

Promotion Time

Promotions are always a time for celebration and since one of our squad members was being promoted to the rank of sergeant, it should be a gala like no other. At least, until we could find another excuse to try and outdo it.

I decided we should take our newly promoted sergeant to the Patapsco Inn in Baltimore county for the party. I called ahead and tipped off the bartender that our newest supervisor was somewhat of a lightweight when it came to drinking. The scheme to get him very fucked up went into play and he would be given shots of whiskey while the rest of us were given soda.

The party went into high gear the instant we arrived at the Patapsco Inn. Of course, it wasn't long before our newly promoted was well on his way to intoxication. So, it was time to call ahead to our next stop and arrange for additional benefits as a way of saying congratulations.

We left the Patapsco Inn and went to a more "exotic" type of establishment where our new sergeant was pounced upon by one of the dancers. Ah, instant party overdrive. He tried to protest, saying he was a married man, but that only encouraged the young lady. He had has tonsils checked frequently, his neck licked and kissed and was treated to several lap dances.

When we left he had an array of glitters in various colors in his hair and eyebrows and they covered his sweater front and back. He reeked of the perfume she had obviously swan in prior to work and we had to take him back to the station so he could shower before going home. While in the shower he mumbled and cursed us for the hangover he was sure to have in the morning and we sympathized by laughing. As far as his sweater, I think he burned that.

Nap Time My Ass

"Thou Shalt Not Sleep on Night Shift." Tis The Eleventh Commandment according to Lieutenant Cogle.

Well, here I am a full of piss and vinegar rookie, fresh out the academy and looking for excitement and adventure. Any kind of excitement and adventure that would lead to the arrest of a murder suspect, or the capture of an armed robber or even a few burglars.

So, it's a night shift and I'm wired for action, but not long out of briefing my Field Training Officer (FTO) tells me to drive to Bill's Towing on Route 40 in Ellicott City. I was curious about the order, but I did as I was told. Immediately after I pulled on to the lot my FTO gets out of the front passenger's seat, opens the backdoor and climbs in. He says, "Just sit here, keep your eyes open and don't do anything." Then he proceeds to take off his shoes and gun belt and stretches out across the back seat and goes to sleep.

Son-of-a-bitch! Here I am all fired up, wanting to see some action and this prick decides to break the 11th Commandment and go to sleep. Not only does he go to sleep, but he also expects me to be his lookout why he bags Zees in the backseat.

I looked around and saw that Old King Cole at the Enchanted Forest across the street and I were the only two keeping watch. It wasn't long before I was ready to scream out of boredom. Then, the emergency tone sounded over the radio and the dispatcher is calling my number.

"Go ahead," I responded with enough enthusiasm for the entire squad.

They advised of a serious accident on U.S. Route 40 several miles east of my location. I immediately had the car in gear and put my foot on the accelerator and jammed it to the floor.

As I was passing 85 miles per hour and headed for 90, I heard a loud screech from behind me. "What the fuck're you doing?"

"Going to a PI," I yelled and kept on going.

I'm trying not to laugh at my FTO who is bouncing around like a rubber ball in the backseat, trying to get his shoes and gun belt on. He's calling me every no good mother in the book, screaming for me to slow down and I pretended to be deaf. A minute later I braked to a stop at the accident and ignored my FTO, making him climb over the front seat to get out of the car. I knew an ass chewing was ahead, but I'd do my best not to chuckle while being chewed.

Life and Times in Law Enforcement
Marty Schoppert

As a young rookie I was entering the police station with my FTO, Miles Alban. It was just after 10 AM and a suspect was being interviewed by two detectives in a room just off the hallway. I heard one ask, "Where were you born?"

"In a room," he answered with a smug laugh.

"Where were you born?"

"In a bed," he said this time.

"Where were you born?"

"In a house," he snorted.

"Okay, let's try this one more time. Where were you born?"

"Oh, besides from my mother," he giggled.

Before the detectives could respond, Miles Alban sticks his head in the door and says, "Did you come out the front or the back?"

The questioning halted for several minutes while attempts were made to restore order and it took me quite a bit longer to write the report I'd come into the station to complete.

Bovine Rain

I was sitting at a major intersection at a stop light on a rather beautiful afternoon, waiting for my light to turn green so I could make a right turn. As I looked to the other side at traffic I noticed a stake-body farm type truck in the left lane. I also immediately saw what appeared to be a stream of liquid about 3 inches or so in width spraying over the top rail of the truck and falling on to the hood of a small car on the truck's right. I knew this type of truck was not used to transport liquids unless they were contained in some type of drum.

The car's driver, upon spotting me across the street, began to frantically wave to me. At about the same time the stream of water stopped and the head of a large cow popped over the top of the rail on the left side of the truck. Immediately, it was all too apparent that the cow, in need of relief did so on to the hood of the car.

Now, the driver seemed to be even more frantic as he waved at me. Not being aware of any crime that had taken place, nor of any statutes, ordinances or laws that made a bovine's relief a crime, and fully realizing that police involvement in natural occurrences are often fruitless, I waved back and, as Mr. Horace Greeley suggested many years ago, hauled ass westward on Route 40.

Technology and Satisfaction

As the Howard County Police Department began to grow, its technical capabilities also grew. A huge step for us was in the radio room with the installation of a new computerized dispatch system that would service the needs, in turn, of three dispatchers.

True sophistication finally arrived when each dispatcher received their very own computer. After the normal required training, the dispatchers were turned loose on the patrol officers.

I recall one of the first days with the new equipment, while one of the department's best dispatchers was happily handling the requests from various officers and dispatching calls. Fortunately, there were no emergencies and the calls were pretty much routine. However, after a time, we became aware that the radio had gone silent. After a somewhat longer than usual time stretch, she tried to return to the air, but quickly cut off. Again, she keyed the mic, but was laughing almost uncontrollably and cut off. Finally, she blurted to all officers,

"Sorry I was off the air. My computer just went down on me."

It's still debated to this day as to whether or not someone in a patrol car whispered, "Need a cigarette break?"

More Bits and Pieces

Contributed by Jim Reske

Yes, I also remember the 11th Commandment: "Thou shalt not sleep on night shift." And it was woe to those who failed to obey and were caught snoozing. That was especially true for the snoozers that were caught by those of us who would go far out of our way to teach a lesson.

And, there on a clear, starlit night opportunity to become the teacher knocked. Certainly, several of us were clamoring to move to the head of the class to be the teacher, but in this particular instance several were required.

An officer was found to be more than snoozing and we made our way to his car with jacks and concrete blocks. We quickly began jacking up his car and in record time had his patrol car sitting on blocks.

It wasn't long before the tone woke him up and he was being sent on a call. He put the car in gear, hit the accelerator and listened to the sounds of wheels spinning faster and faster. When he finally realized he was going nowhere, he knew what had happened. And, rather than call for assistance in getting his car off the blocks, he quietly toiled away until he was back in service.

One of our female officers also tempted fate and closed her eyes. While she was cuddling with the sandman, the red and blue covers were removed from her emergency lights.

Almost immediately she was dispatched to an emergency call. She turned on her overheads and discovered only bright white lights instead of the red and blue.

Then there was a young man, Butch, who decided to take his shoes off and nap. He awoke to find his shoes gone and had to walk into the station in stocking feet and explain why.

There is also a story of a Maryland State Trooper who was in an out of the way spot and thought to be asleep. The driver's side window was down and someone thought it would be fun to sneak up and scare the shit out of him.

He actually got down on his hands and knees and crawled up to the car and to the driver's door. He moved to a crouching position and very slowly began rising up to scare the Trooper. He had risen to the point where his nose was just above the window opening. All of a sudden the barrel of a gun was pressed firmly against the tip of his nose.

"I don't know who the fuck you are," the Trooper snarled without looking to see who it was. "But, you'd better slither back down the side of my car and disappear."

It was said that the joker vanished in near record time.

UFO Reports

I remember an officer by the name of John Dennis who was a firm believer in Alien existence and was certain that sooner or later they would appear. I mean he was so hardcore in his belief that he carried a small suitcase with extra clothing just in case they arrived while he was working.

Naturally, there were a number of John's fellow officers who thought he should have his beliefs proven true.

Paul Hajek and a few of his trusted friends managed to get a hold of a weather balloon. They waited for the next night shift and took the balloon to Lake Elkhorn, fixed a light inside and sent it into the night sky. Of course, they had it tethered with a long, heavy-duty cord so they could control its movements.

Next, John was dispatched to check on suspicious lights over Lake Elkhorn. When he reached Lake Elkhorn he thought the Aliens were at last going to make contact. He ran and grabbed his camera and began shooting some pictures.

Paul Hajek "arrived" and said he wasn't going to take any chances and was going to open fire on the object because it was now getting closer.

John went nuts, screaming that this was no way to greet alien visitors. Of course, when "The UFO" hit the surface of the lake and floated to shore, he found that it was only a weather balloon. I think he was pissed off for a month over that prank.

The Car Accident

Frank Becker was dispatched to investigate an accident on Town and Country Boulevard. He pulled up behind the cars involved and began his investigation. After gathering facts and collecting drivers licenses and registrations, he returned to his car to start his report.

Somewhere about midway through his report, a woman was travelling down T&C Boulevard and rear-ended his cruiser.

Frank got on the radio, "Headquarters, my car has just been hit by a woman on T&C, send the area supervisor to my location."

With that he looked in the rearview mirror and saw that she was backing up. She stopped momentarily and started toward his car.

He grabbed the mic and yelled, "Holy shit! The bitch's is gonna hit me again."

Swim Meet

In the early days we were having an evening swimming party at the Town and Country Pool.

As the beer flowed and the evening progressed, some in the party decided to toss Leo Dodge into the pool. They dragged him to the side of the pool and hoisted him into the air. And, all the while Leo is yelling, "I can't swim."

SPLASH!

Damn! Leo really couldn't swim.

One of the pranksters turned lifeguard, jumped in and pulled him out.

Pistol Range

The 3rd Platoon was at the Lake Linganore range for a highly anticipated training day. After a morning of practice it was decided to set up a "Shoot/Don't Shoot" scenario.

The targets were placed after all of us were told to stand out behind the gate. We were then called in one at a time and "ran the gauntlet."

Dave Richards, the designated Range Master, took his badge from its case and attached it to one of the targets. Well, it was dark gold against a black background and somewhat difficult to see. But, we were expected to use good judgment, have excellent observation skills and determine friend from foe.

Bill Seifert stepped through the gate and immediately blasted the first target. He moved down the line as instructed, quickly spun left and fired. He made what Dave Richards called a "One in million shot." The bullet hit Dave's badge dead center.

Dave shrugged and laughed. "At least I wasn't wearing it."

The Quartermaster's comment regarding replacement of the badge: "Tell me again how this happened."

Phone Sex

The briefing room in our old police headquarters on Fels Lane in Ellicott City wasn't exactly a spacious penthouse sitting room. There were tables for report writing, vending machines, filing cabinets, chairs and a desk or two for the Patrol Supervisors to share.

It was just after 1400 hours and a few officers were already straggling in for the evening shift briefing, which began at 1500. A supervisor was at one of the desks reviewing reports and two or three detectives were standing at the back of the room near the vending machines discussing a case.

Officer Woody Rush walked in the back door and sat down at one of the tables. A moment or two later he picked up a phone and dialed a number.

Naturally, due to the size of the room there was no such thing as a private conversation.

A few seconds later everyone in the room overheard, "Yes, ma'am, this is Officer Rush from the Howard County Police."

There was a somewhat lengthy pause and Woody said, "Yes, Ma'am, I've called to discuss a Penis Erecti. Yes, ma'am, that's Latin for hard-on."

Of course, everybody damn near fell out of their chairs, the detectives stopped talking and the supervisor put his pen down and stared at Woody.

After a second or two, Woody looked around the room and smiled. "I'm on hold."

Fingerprint Insanity

I'm certain Howard Cogle has been mentioned a few times, but I'm not sure how well he was described.

Howard is not a small person—not by any standard. He was at least 6'6" in height and, in his prime, was about 235-240 pounds of very solid human being. He quietly confessed to some that he worked out on a regular basis—not to be a body builder, but to stay in shape. He is also a very patient man with an outrageous sense of humor and is not easily intimidated or pissed off.

I happened to be in the Fels Lane station when Howard came in with a prisoner. He took the man to the fingerprint station outside of the briefing room, inked his fingers and rolled his prints and then completed the task with a set of palm prints.

At that time the only place to clean up afterward was upstairs in the men's restroom. He was in the process of telling his prisoner where they would have to go to wash, when the man ran his hands down the front of Howard's light blue uniform shirt.

I saw this guy go up the stairs, with an assist from Howard, and I don't believe his feet ever touched a single step.

Rookie Rip Off

Our police academy rookies were assigned to their respective platoons and, as always, we could see the looks of anticipation on their faces when they arrived for their first days in "the real world." They were immediately the focus of many verbal barbs from the "old salts" and our group seemed to take them in stride.

We were working an evening shift, and they had been with us only a day or two, when Tommy Watkins was dispatched to check for an injured deer on Route 108 just east of Route 29.

He arrived at the location and found the deer, which had been injured and would have to be destroyed. In most instances an injured deer was put out of its misery with a shot to the back of the head with our issued service revolver. Tommy was about to draw his weapon when another officer arrived with his rookie.

They approached Tommy and after a little idle chatter, he looked at the rookie and said, "Is that a brand new revolver?"

"Yes, sir," the rookie replied.

"Mind if I take a look at it?" Tommy said. "I still have this old, used one they issued me and I'd just like to see a new one up close."

A moment later the rookie carefully drew his weapon and passed it to Tommy. He looked it over and commented how nice it felt to hold a new weapon. A second later he turned around, walked over to the deer and, with the rookie's revolver, shot it twice in the head. Then he casually strolled back to the rookie, handed him his revolver and said, "Don't forget to clean it and tomorrow when you report for duty, stop by the Quartermaster's office and pick up two bullets."

The Manhole – Take One
Frank Dawson in the lead role

Night shift for the 4th Platoon and Frank Dawson was on his assigned Patrol Beat in what was then Sector 9 in Columbia. He exited Route 29 and began driving on Snowden River Parkway.

"I had a speeding driver almost instantly," Frank said. "So, I turned on my overheads, flashed the high beams and he pulled over to the left into the grass median.

"I stopped my car behind him, got out and started walking up to his car. Of course, I'm trying to do everything by the book safety wise. I'm watching the driver, looking to see if anybody else is in the car with him, keeping an eye out for any sudden movements on his part and…

"Son-of-a-bitch! Some asshole had removed the cover from a manhole and I stepped right in. Now, here I am scrabbling to get my ass out and wondering if the guy is still up there, or did he drive off.

"Finally, I climb out and I'm pissed. Well, the guy's still there and I walked up and introduced myself and asked for his license and registration."

"Yes, sir," he replied. Then he said, "I saw you walking up and all of a sudden you disappeared. What happened?"

"Without thinking, I blurted I fell in a fuckin' manhole.

"Well, the guy busts out laughing and now I'm really pissed

off. I grabbed his license and registration and went back to my car and wrote his ass a summons."

Naturally, Frank was told by more than one fellow officer and his supervisor, that writing the guy was a bad move. This was one man who was surely going to appear for trail. And, sure enough, he did.

Frank very professionally testified to pacing the car, making the stop and writing the driver a summons for exceeding the posted speed limit.

When it came time for the defendant to testify, the first words out of his mouth were, "Your Honor, the only reason that Officer Dawson wrote me a ticket is that he was upset because he fell in a manhole."

The entire courtroom erupted into fits of laughter and when calm and order was finally restored, the judge looked at Frank and said, "Officer Dawson, is it true that you fell into a manhole?"

"Yes, Your Honor."

"Case dismissed."

The Manhole – Take Two
Frank Dawson in the lead with Sergeant Lee Hajek in a supporting role

Once again it's the night shift for the 4th Platoon and as soon as Frank Dawson calls in service, the dispatcher tells him to respond to a report of an open manhole on Rogers Avenue.

Frank arrived at the location given along with Sergeant Lee Hajek. After a brief search they found the open manhole, but no cover. They began checking the area and eventually climbed a hill, which had a fairly steep grade. At the top of the hill they discovered the manhole cover and decided they could carry it down the hill and put back in its proper place. That is until they tried to lift it.

When they realized that attempting to pick it up and carry it down the hill was futile, Lee suggested they could stand it on its edge and roll it down. Together, she and Frank managed to stand it up and began slowly moving it to the top of the hill.

When they reached the downward crest, gravity took over and the manhole cover slipped from their grasp and took off down the hill.

"That fuckin' thing was picking up speed and heading right for my car," Frank said. "Son-of-a-bitch! Right into my fuckin' door. It caved the whole thing in."

Lee laughed and said, "Well, we at least got the cover back where it belonged."

Of course, the humor she found in the situation quickly evaporated when she discovered how much paperwork would be required to explain the damage to the cruiser.

On the other hand, Frank didn't find it funny at all and he cursed the gods of misfortune for days.

The Manhole – Take Three
Frank Dawson once again in a starring role with
Officer Larry Horn and the 4th Platoon in supporting roles

Yes, it's the night shift again for the 4th Platoon, but Frank is sitting out his patrol duties while assigned to the radio room. His assignment to the radio room came about due to a nasty knee injury suffered while dancing. Naturally, with Frank the injury was severe enough to require him to utilize crutches for walking.

It was the last night of the shift and the entire platoon was going to breakfast the following morning. Frank said the only bright spot of the night was looking forward to being with everybody at breakfast.

As the night wore on, Larry discovered a construction site with hundreds of manhole covers stacked in neat rows. He waited until 0500 and returned to the site and located the foreman for the job.

Larry told him about Frank and his inclination to find chaos and madness centered around manholes and manhole covers. The foreman found his tale hilarious and, after a bit of smooth talking by

Larry helped him load a manhole cover into the police cruiser.

In no time at all Larry was at the station and parked beside Frank's personal car. With a little help from a friend, the manhole cover was placed on the right front seat of Frank's car.

By the time everyone secured from the shift, they knew that a manhole cover was in Frank's car.

When their paperwork was completed, they hurried into the office space of the Criminal Investigations Division to hide and complete the prank.

Frank left the radio room at 0800 and walked into the report writing area and was surprised to find only Sergeant Lilley there completing his review of the reports.

"Sarge, what happened to everybody? I thought we were going to breakfast together."

"I guess they left already."

"Are they pissed at me? I mean, I thought they were going to wait for me."

"You'll hafta ask them, Frank."

When the last report was signed and dropped off, Sergeant Lilley said, "Come on, Frank, I'll walk out with you."

Outside on the walk, or more appropriately, the limp to his car, Frank expressed his fears that the platoon was pissed off at him for some reason. But, his concerns vanished the moment he was close enough to see the manhole cover on the front seat of his car.

At the same instant, the blinds in the CID office went up and he turned around to see his "friends" laughing and clapping.

Later, the manhole cover found its way to Frank's Columbia apartment. There, sitting atop three cinderblocks, it served as a coffee table.

Frank swears that he still has the manhole cover in his home in Westminster, Maryland.

Snake Charmer
Detective Paul Hajek in the lead role with a
faux reptile and an anonymous detective as supporting cast.

Paul Hajek and several other detectives and patrol officers had arrested four young men from Baltimore City for shoplifting at the Columbia Mall.

Try as he would, Paul couldn't get one of them to confess to the crime. Even when confronted with the recovered stolen clothing, they continued to deny involvement in the theft.

It was getting on to late afternoon and Paul had a suspect in the CID office trying to get him to admit to the crimes. There was no such thing as an interview room in the station on Fels Lane and most talks with suspects were conducted in the office. It was a rare day indeed when you could find privacy to talk with suspects and witnesses alike.

Paul was talking with the suspect when another detective arrived for his afternoon shift.

He immediately noticed the piles of clothing stacked atop the filing cabinets, each labeled with the names of the respective stores the items had been stolen from. He listened for several minutes to Paul explaining to the suspect that he was caught with the stolen items in his possession and should just admit to his part in the crime. But the young man wouldn't budge.

The suspect's back was to the newly arrived detective and didn't notice that he'd opened his desk drawer and removed an item. A few moments later the detective placed a very life like snake in a stack of blue jeans. The mouth of the snake was open, displaying two rows of teeth and its tongue protruded about two to three inches.

It was hanging about a foot directly above the suspect's head and the tongue was wiggling as the head moved slightly in an up and down motion.

Paul didn't smile or lose a beat. He said, "And you guys just couldn't stick to stealing clothes. You had to go and rip off the pet store too."

"We didn't rip off no pet store."

Paul nodded as he glanced above the suspect's head. "Yeah, you did."

The suspect turned, looking up over his shoulder. He let out a wall shaking scream as he jumped out of the chair.

A second later he was yelling, "Man, we stole the goddamn clothes, but I swear we didn't steal no fuckin' snake."

By the time he sat down again the snake was nowhere to be found.

A few minutes later, Paul was like a priest hearing Saturday afternoon confessions. The suspect was rattling off details of the thefts one after another.

Paul said, "After a while I think he was confessing to crimes he hadn't even committed yet."

The Legend of Robert "Sweet Bobby" Moore

Robert W. Moore, a man known by such nicknames as "Sweet Bobby, The Animal, The Lizard and Sweetness," is a former Marine, Baltimore City, and Howard County, Maryland Police Officer. Oftentimes it is difficult to find just the right words to describe Bob. A human being who seemed impervious to pain, and a man many described as possessing the strength of a Grizzly Bear. Bob is a man that, if for some reason during a moment of complete insanity, you harbored a notion that you'd like to try and kick his ass, you'd better do so from behind. Of course, if that urge overcame you, you should be armed with a sledgehammer or a tractor-trailer, and pray to God that your assault didn't simply piss him off.

Sweetness was known far and wide for a most notorious trademark—his laugh, a laugh that seemed to rise up from within the depths of his being. A very deep "heh, heh, heh." And, that "heh, heh, heh" always seemed to come out of him at the most peculiar times—like when someone pulled a gun on him, or threatened to kick his ass.

Stories surrounding Bob's exploits were told over and over in restaurants, bars, around dinner tables, in homes and on many street corners. Some listened in awe, while others didn't believe the fables, but those who knew the truth, admired Bob's bravado and held him near and dear in their hearts. Police officers under his command were comfortable knowing he would stand by them in good times and bad. And, police officers facing danger always prayed that he would be nearby, or on the way to help them. As for me, I'm happy and proud to say I've called Bob my friend for over 48 years.

The tales of Robert "The Animal" Moore are from another era. Restless times of race riots, flag and draft card burning. A time when young men marched off to war in a place called Vietnam, and came home to jeers instead of a hero's welcome. Indeed, it was a time when the legend of "Sweet Bobby" grew to be as real as the morning sunrise.

Motor Vehicle Matrimony

The County Seat of Howard County, Ellicott City, long held a reputation as *the* place where you could just drop by any time, day or night, and get married. People would travel from New York and even Florida in search of a Justice of the Peace, or minister to join them in wedlock. Yet, much to their dismay, those giddy travellers soon found Ellicott City's renown to be nothing more than a myth.

It was an unusually boring Friday evening and Bob was assigned the task of Night Shift Duty Officer. He had just settled down behind the desk to look over a stack of paperwork when a taxicab stopped in front of the police station. After a few minutes a couple stumbled from the backseat and staggered, arm in arm, toward the front door of the building. Somehow they managed to make it to the desk, where they announced very loudly to Bob, "We're in love and wanna get married."

Suddenly the lobby was filled with coughs, guffaws, chokes and a round of not so discreet comments.

"Man, you've gotta be kidding. She's so ugly she has to back up to a glass of water to get a drink," one of the officers said.

She giggled, and the man explained that he had been at sea for months as a Merchant Marine. Soon after returning to port he collected his pay, which was rather substantial, and set out to quench his thirst. He located a "respectable" establishment on Baltimore's world famous Block, and began to wash away all those months of loneliness.

Somewhere between his first drink and mild intoxication, the woman of his dreams came in and sat down beside him. "It was love at first sight," he said to Bob. After several rounds of drinks to celebrate finding true love, they decided to marry.

"Jesus, she's so ugly she'd make a train take a dirt road," someone said from behind him. "You can't be serious about marrying her."

He attempted to stand up straight. "I'm in love with this woman and I wanna marry her."

Bob leaned back in his chair, nodded and smiled. "Look, why don't you just go to a motel and spend the night? Get to know each other a little better, if you know what I mean? If you're still in love in the morning, then make arrangements to get married."

The man shook his head. "No. I wanna do the right thing. I don't wanna make love to this woman until we're man and wife."

Bob explained that they could no longer drive to Ellicott City and get married on the spur of the moment. They hung their heads, and seemed on the verge of tears when a very mischievous twinkle appeared in Bob's eyes. "I can help you, though."

"Really," the man said. "How?"

"I have the authority to perform a temporary marriage ceremony." A few officers scurried laughing into a nearby men's room. "But, you've gotta remember this is only a temporary marriage. It's good only until eight o'clock Monday morning. After that, if you decide that you still wanna be married, you'll hafta apply for a license, find a minister and have another ceremony."

Of course, the loving couple was elated and agreed to be temporarily joined in wedded bliss. Bob opened the restroom door and summoned two officers to stand as witnesses while he joined the happy couple in holy matrimony. With witnesses holding their breath beside the blushing couple, Bob reached into the desk and pulled out a copy of the Maryland Motor Vehicle Code. Adjusting his ascot, and with a rather official flair, he opened the book, appropriately it seemed to the section prohibiting reckless driving.

In a world record ceremony, Bob pronounced them man and wife, but would take one last step to make everything seem more official. He called Officer Wayne Ridgely to the station and told him to give the newly weds a police escort to a motel. Wayne grinned, and a moment later with lights flashing and siren wailing he escorted the taxicab to Brown's Motel on U. S. Route 40.

When the siren faded in the distance, Bob sat down. "Heh, heh, heh. When that guy wakes up in the morning, it's gonna be bad enough that he'll probably have the worst hangover in his entire life. But, when he rolls over and sees his bride, I bet he'll run all the way to the bay bridge and jump off the top span."

The Howard Place Chainsaw Massacre

The Howard Place was a local hangout noted for its good food, cold drinks, and live entertainment. The clientele was a mix of varying backgrounds from lawyers, police officers, and college students to construction workers. Everybody got along well and enjoyed sitting around the bar or tables talking, sharing a drink, listening to music and dancing.

"Sweet Bobby" was a regular visitor to the Howard Place, and usually stopped by for a steak and a cold drink. Mind you, Bob was very particular in the way he wanted his steak prepared. "I want a steak, very, very tender and very, very rare. Have the steer walk by the fire and cut off a slice." And, he meant every word of it.

One evening, after a long day of cutting down trees and stacking firewood, Bob stopped by for a steak dinner. There was an unusually large crowd there for a weekday, but the band playing that evening had a huge following. Bob sat down at the bar beside Officer Robert Reid, and gave his order to the bartender. He looked over at Reid after placing his order and said, "I probably should've just ordered the whole steer. I really worked up an appetite out there today."

Ronnie Jones, the owner of the Howard Place, was seated to Bob's right and was there when the dinner order arrived. Within a matter of seconds "Sweetness" complained to him that the steak was very tough. Jones, of course, disagreed, saying it was merely Bob's over-active imagination.

"Hell, I couldn't cut this thing with my chainsaw."

Reid wouldn't dare let the moment pass. "Moore, you ain't got a hair on your ass if you don't get your chainsaw and prove it."

Bob left the bar as the band began playing its second set of the evening. Moments later he returned to the bar carrying a large chainsaw. Certainly nobody really believed the grinning, man-bear holding the saw would really fire it up and cut the steak. They stared in disbelief as he cranked up the saw and began attacking the steak. Smoke belched out and began filling the restaurant and bar. Soon, French-fries, lettuce, tomato and steak were flying around the bar. The band stopped playing, and the crowd started to laugh and cheer Bob on as he continued his assault on the steak.

"Christ, Bob, shut it off. I'll get you another steak," Ronnie Jones screamed over the roar of the chainsaw.

Bob stopped the saw, put it against the wall and sat down. He glanced over at Reid. "Heh, heh, heh."

A few minutes later his second steak arrived—very, very, rare and very, very tender.

The Family Reunion

Family reunions certainly are not uncommon, but in some instances they turn out much differently than anticipated. Such was the case of a family get together held in Western Howard County. Relatives from Tennessee, Kentucky, North Carolina and points south gathered to get reacquainted. To be sure, there were ample containers of alcoholic beverages to wash down the barbecue and other foods.

Everyone in law enforcement knows that consumption of alcohol bolsters courage, lowers inhibitions, and often creates what is known as "beer muscles," causing some to believe they can whip Superman. At this reunion it was the women who first "flexed" their newly found beer muscles, and a catfight ensued.

Initially, the men were satisfied to cheer on the female combatants, but the inevitable punch was thrown, and all hell broke loose.

The host of the gathering, unable to quell the ever-growing brawl, called police. The first to arrive was Officer Richard Doxen, and upon seeing the size of the melee, he called for assistance. A familiar voice crackled over the radio and Corporal Robert "The Animal" Moore was on his way.

He arrived, looked the situation over, laughed and shook his head. He tried the PA system from the car, and the horn to get the attention of the fighters. Finally he turned on the siren, but the brawl continued. It was obvious to Bob and Officer Doxen that they were not going to be able to restore order—at least not in the conventional sense. And, it was just about this time that a very large, mangy cat wandered through the field of battle and settled atop the woodpile.

Bob turned to the homeowner. "Is that your cat?"

"No, it's some stray that showed up here, and the damn thing's been nothin' but trouble since it got here."

Bob grinned. "Heh, heh, heh."

In those days not much was said about the side arms worn on duty. Although the standard issued weapon at the time was the Smith and Wesson .38 Caliber Revolver, Bob was toting a Smith and Wesson .44 Magnum. He was lugging the original version of the "Dirty Harry" Model with the 6½-inch barrel. While the family fight continued to grow, Bob drew the cannon from its holster. And, as casually as though standing on the firing line at the pistol range, he took aim and blew the cat off the woodpile.

The roar of the big magnum rose well above the din of the battle and immediately caught everyone's attention. Pugilists and wrestlers alike stopped and turned their heads in the direction of the grinning policeman, who still clutched the smoking cannon in his right hand.

With silence now hovering over the field of conflict, Bob bellowed, "Now, what the hell's the matter?"

Without uttering so much as a single word, the former

antagonists were quickly seated side by side, eating beef, drinking beer and engaging in somewhat pleasant conversation. Soon, Bob holstered his revolver and walked back to his car. He looked over at the host. "Heh, heh, heh. I thought you had a fight here. I don't see a fight, do you?"

The host turned to Officer Doxen and muttered, "Sweet Jesus Christ. Nobody in their right mind's gonna fight with that crazy son-of-a-bitch runnin' around loose."

The Xerox Phantom

When word began circulating that the Howard County Police Department was thinking of replacing its copy machine, companies quickly beat a path to the door, hoping to get the contract. Each offered a copy machine, free of charge, for up to a full week to demonstrate its capabilities. The game of One-ups-man-ship began in earnest, and finally Xerox delivered a machine, the likes of which nobody in the department had ever before seen. This copier offered some eye raising features, and the salesman boasted that it could make prints from 8½ x 11 up to poster-sized copies. None other than Corporal Robert "The Lizard" Moore, the Night Shift Duty Officer, would immediately put the Xerox boast to the test.

The following morning, police officers, radio dispatchers and secretaries arriving for work were warned that The Xerox Phantom had struck sometime during the night. Copies of an "unknown" party's buttocks were on display everywhere. From restrooms, to desk drawers, to holding cells and the radio room, The Phantom's cheeks were bared in various sizes.

Chief of Police, Russ Walters opened the door to his office and was greeted with a poster-sized copy of the mystery cheeks, which were tacked prominently above and behind his chair.

Scrawled in red letters, with a red arrow pointing downward were the words, "KISS MY."

Chief Walters hurried back into the lobby and shouted, "There's a copy of somebody's ass hangin' behind my desk."

It was almost an hour before a somewhat normal order returned to the police station. And, it was at that time one of the secretaries noticed that just below the "eye-catching" cheeks was just a hint of shorts, which displayed cute little valentine hearts.

Bob winked at the secretary. "Guess I'll hafta go home and burn my shorts."

But, before leaving, Bob had one last thing to do. It was one of those temptations that no matter the level of self-discipline, he just had to do it. He knocked on the door and stuck his head into office of Russ Walters and said, "Chief, you gonna call for a line-up to see if you can ID the culprit?"

"Moore, get your ass outta my office and go home."

Come Blow Your Horn

Bob began his law enforcement career in the City of Baltimore, Maryland, and it was there that the legend of "Sweet Bobby Moore" began to take shape. On a steamy, sweltering summer afternoon, he was ending his tour of duty and thinking of nothing but leaving the city and finding peace and quiet and some relief from the brutal heat. The thought of sitting in the shade with a cold drink seemed like a good idea. He got behind the wheel of his '56 Chevy and headed out Franklin Street and its endless maze of traffic signals. Minding his own business, he followed the steadily growing stream of commuters west toward the county. Not long into his trek he noticed a car rapidly bearing down on him, and suddenly it seemed as if it was glued to his bumper. Try as he might, he just couldn't get the car off his rear end.

"I really think the son-of-a-bitch was trying to get in the back seat," Bob would later say.

In no time at all, the man behind him wasn't satisfied with simply tailgating. He began to blow his horn—not now and then, but constantly, and especially at traffic lights. The very instant a traffic signal turned green, he laid on the horn. Bob was beginning to steam under the collar, and when he began to boil, it was time to get out of his way.

For those who knew him, it was easy to read the telltale sign that "Sweetness" was starting to get riled. Bob's skin would change color, and the deep red would rise in his neck. Like a temperature gauge, you could read his degree of agitation. The higher the red climbed, the more pissed off he was becoming. When red hit the tops of his ears, he had been pushed beyond his limit of endurance and his tormentor was going to endure the wrath of "The Animal."

The man continued to hammer the horn, and the incessant "honk, honk, honk" had taken its toll on Bob. His temperature gauge had reached its boiling point, and he wouldn't tolerate another minute of this aggravating man and his honking horn. He stopped at the next red traffic signal and waited. The light turned green and, right on cue, the man slammed his hand down on the horn. Instead of driving on, Bob turned off the engine and got out of his car. An instant later he was walking toward his source of irritation, and the man had no place to go. He was hemmed in by the evening traffic.

Bob didn't confront the driver, at least not immediately. He paused and opened the hood of the man's car, reached down with his bear sized hands, wrapped them around the horns and ripped them from the car. It was a certainty that the look on his face was sending a very clear message to the man behind the wheel as he walked to the driver's door. He shoved the horns through the open window and held them just inches from the man's face. A moment later he dropped them in his lap and said, "Here, blow 'em now."

The man was still sitting at the traffic light as Bob drove away smiling, and surely enjoying some of the peace and quiet he'd been daydreaming of.

Traffic Stop to Gunfire

On a Friday evening, Bob was patrolling the roads of West Friendship in Howard County, approaching the intersection of Sandhill Road. He watched a car roll through the Stop Sign and speed up, kicking up gravel and squealing wheels. Bob thought he'd stop the car, write the driver a warning, and send him on his way. When he activated the overhead lights, the driver accelerated and raced westward along Frederick Road to Route 32.

At the intersection he turned left, cutting off several cars, hoping to elude his pursuer. He had travelled almost a mile when he cut sharply to his right and began fleeing down a narrow dirt road. Bob was right on his bumper as they bounced over the unpaved surface toward the parking lot of a private club. The car slid to a stop and the driver jumped out, but was surprised to find Bob already blocking his path to the club's entrance.

Bob immediately recognized the man, and knew he had no respect whatsoever for police officers. But, he followed protocol to the letter, and asked for the man's driver's license and registration. A heartbeat later, Bob found himself looking into the barrel of a small caliber handgun. He didn't even blink. Instead he looked the man squarely in the eyes and smiled. "Heh, heh, heh. You don't really think you're gonna kill me with that, do you?"

Bob's actions and comments must have caused the man to have second thoughts. For a moment he seemed puzzled, and then, for some unknown reason, he turned the gun and stared at it. In those seconds of uncertainty, the "Bear in Blue" pounced with the quickness of a cat.

Bob hurled the man to the ground and tore the gun from his hands. A ham-sized fist crashed into the side of the man's head a half dozen times, knocking him senseless.

When Bob looked up, he found that a crowd of more than a hundred people surrounded him, and many of them were friends of the man lying at his feet. What he did next would be considered nothing short of complete insanity, but he grinned. Then he leaned over, grasped the front of the man's jacket and pulled his head from the ground.

"Wanna hear what your gun sounds like?" he growled. With that he took the man's gun, held it close to his right ear and fired. "Would you like to hear it again?" He held it beside his left ear and fired again. "Heh, heh, heh. How'd it sound?" He fired two more shots, one beside each ear.

Glancing over his shoulder, he found that the crowd had moved a considerable distance away from him. He rolled the man over, handcuffed him and stuffed him in the back of his cruiser as other police officers began arriving.

Without coaxing, the majority of the crowd went back inside

to continue partying. Those who remained outside laughed, and talked with police officers about a crazy son-of-a-bitch that had fired shots.

In the end, the man who pulled the gun on "Sweetness" was sentenced to six months in the county jail. At the trial there was no mention of the shots that had been fired, and no one filed a formal complaint, or made so much as a single telephone call about what happened that night.

Tonight's Menu – Duck

In its early days, Columbia, Maryland was still a very rural area, consisting of thousands of acres of working farmland and other undeveloped land. It was late afternoon when I was dispatched to a call for an alarm on telephone company equipment shack. I drove off the main highway (Route 29) and along a dirt road, searching for the shack. I drove along streams, through fields and wooded areas before locating the source of the alarm.

I had just determined that everything was okay, when Bob drove up. We talked for a minute and began driving back toward Route 29. As I was passing a small pond, which was surrounded by trees and heavy brush, I spotted two Mallard ducks on the water. I didn't say anything over the radio, but I pointed out the window at the ducks.

Almost immediately I heard, "Twenty-five, back up" come over my radio. In my rear-view mirror I could see "Sweetness" already getting out of his car as I put mine in reverse. A few seconds later I was standing beside him.

"Heh, heh, heh. Sure looks like duck for Wednesday night's dinner," he said, drawing his revolver. "I'll get the one on the left. You take the one on the right."

I was thinking, *we're not really gonna do this, are we?* But, I was standing beside Bob, revolver in hand and taking aim at the duck on the right.

"Heh, hch, heh. On three," he said. "One, two, three."

Instantly there was a volley of gunfire and so many times, although we were expert shots, I wonder how in the hell we nailed both ducks with a hail of bullets from our Smith and Wesson, 4" barrelled revolvers.

A "heh, heh, heh" later, they were in an empty flare box and Bob was saying, "Wild rice and vegetables sound okay for side dishes?"

A Case of Mistaken Identity

The four men passing by Parker's Drive-in on U. S. Route 40 were certain the policeman with the reddish-blonde hair, standing on the parking lot, was the one they had been searching for. They had a grudge to settle and figured this was a perfect time. After all, they had him outnumbered. They parked their car, and a moment later began their attack on him. Almost immediately it was evident that they had jumped the wrong man.

The only similarity between this policeman and the one they'd been searching for was the reddish-blonde hair and his height of five feet ten inches. This man in blue weighed 210 pounds plus and had a fist the size of a Smithfield Ham, or the hoof of a full-grown Clydesdale. Then there was this very strange laugh he had.

They were stunned that he actually laughed when they pounced on him, screaming they were going to kick his ass. Very soon they found themselves on the wrong side of the ass kicking.

Maryland State Trooper Pete Edge was dispatched to assist a Howard County Officer who was fighting four men. He skidded to a stop on the parking lot of Parker's Drive-in, leaped out of his car and stopped in his tracks. Indeed, there was a policeman there, but he was rather handily pummelling the snot out of three men. He stopped beating the three men long enough to look over at Pete and say, "Can I help you?"

Pete shrugged. "I was told you needed help?"

"Heh, heh, heh. I don't need any help." And, with that, Bob proceeded to pound away on the three men again.

"I was really thinking about leaving, when all of a sudden somebody reached out from under a car and grabbed my legs. I looked down and here's a guy with cuts all over his face and a bloody nose, and now he's wrapping his arms around my legs," Pete laughed. "I tried to shake him off, but he wouldn't let go. That's when I realized this guy had to be the fourth suspect."

As Pete tried to pry him from his legs, the man kept yelling, "Help! It's not that animal that needs help. It's us. Please don't leave. Help! Help us."

Driver Training

It was late afternoon when Corporal Bill Brooks parked his State Police cruiser on the side lot of the Howard County Police Station.

As soon as he walked into the building he was greeted by Sweet Bobby and soon a few of the usual barbs and zingers were exchanged before Bill headed to the records division to pick up a report.

Of course, regardless of who was ahead when the exchange between Brooks and Bob ended, Bob was going to have the last laugh.

Bill picked up the report he needed and on his way out the door called to Bob. "If I never see your sorry ass again, it'll be too damn soon."

Bob's response, "Heh, heh, heh."

Brooks drove from Ellicott City to the State Police Barrack at Waterloo during the height of rush hour traffic. Every now and then someone would pull up beside him at a traffic signal, look over and give him a questioning look. He thought nothing of it until he arrived at the barrack, got out of his car and walked toward the front door.

Just a few steps beyond his rear bumper, something caught his eye. He stopped and yelled. "Moore, you no good son-of-a-bitch."

Attached to the rear of his car was a very official sign, which read: Student Driver.

The Other Side

During his career Bob often seemed larger than life, and was a hero to so many who knew him, because he dared to stand his ground when others would flee. He gave no quarter when it came to enforcing the law, and firmly believed it was for everyone, rich or poor, black or white.

There was another side to Bob that only a select few had the opportunity to see. I was blessed to be one of those few. He would go out of his way to help children, regardless of their age. They just seemed to always sense that the smiling, bear-like man had a heart of gold, and I am certain they knew that he would always watch out for them.

There was an occasion many years ago when I attended a Sunday morning Judo exhibition at a local health club. Bob, who had earned a Black Belt in the art of Judo while in Japan, was invited to attend and participate if time allowed.

The man who was demonstrating various throwing techniques had chosen a boy, 15 years of age, and far less skilled than he, to be his partner. Early on it was evident that this man was using the youngster as nothing more than a dummy for the purpose of showing off to the large number of women in attendance. Each time the boy landed hard on the mat, it seemed to bolster the man's already over inflated ego. I looked at Bob and knew he detested what the man was doing. With every new assault by the man on the almost defenceless 15-year-old, I saw Bob's thermometer glow a brighter shade of red. All of a sudden, as the man continued his unmerciful thrashing of the boy, he began to shoot verbal insults at Bob. I don't know what possessed him to do it, but after a number of slurs, he invited Bob to step out and take the boy's place.

Although this man was a head taller and clearly had a greater reach advantage, the moment Bob stared into his eyes he knew he'd made a grave mistake. Try as he might, he couldn't escape the wrath of the enraged Grizzly. Bob threw him around the mat as though he was nothing more than a paper doll. When he slammed him to the mat for the final time, Bob dropped like a rock on top of him and choked him unconscious. As Bob left the mat, the young boy nodded and bowed to him.

"Sweetness" flashed him a big grin as he walked over, patted him on the back and returned his bow.

When he wasn't watching out for the local kids, or protecting the citizens of Howard County, Bob pursed his long time favorite hobby, hunting. He was an avid hunter, who not only hunted locally, but also various states across the country. But his hunting skills weren't used merely to fill his freezer with game, or bag a trophy. He put meat on the tables of many less fortunate people, but never made his efforts known and, in fact, was just as happy helping others without the fanfare.

There is a small group of us who know the value and meaning of true friendship, and the days we spent acting as Guardian Angels for each other. We still find time to share with Bob and a few of our brothers from bygone days, and reminisce of high-speed chases, close calls, and friends who left us too soon. We laugh over a drink while spinning those yarns of "Sweet Bobby," our daring exploits and a few astounding deeds. When it's time to part, there's a round of handshakes and hugs, and the satisfaction of knowing we've held a friendship that's lasted a lifetime.

As for enemies, and as is the case with all of us, only the passing of time seems capable of wearing down the bear of a man so many of us know as "Sweet Bobby." I've often tried to picture his Lord and Maker knocking and announcing, "Okay, Sweetness, it's time to come home." And I can't help but imagine Bob smiling, turning out the light, closing the door, and responding, "Heh, heh, heh."

www.ingramcontent.com/pod-product-compliance
Lightning Source LLC
Chambersburg PA
CBHW051903170526
45168CB00001B/223